*The First Teacher of the Deaf
in the Philippines*

The Life Story of

Mother

Delight Rice

and Her Children

RONALD M. HIRANO

Authored and designed by Ronald M. Hirano

Edited by T.S. Writing Services, LLC
www.tswriting.com

Published by Savory Words Publishing, LLC
www.savorywords.com

ISBN 978-0-9884070-0-8

Printed in the United States of America

*For Deaf and blind children
and their families,
in memory of Delight Rice*

Contents

Dedication iii

Mission vi

Preface
    Ronald M. Hirano vii

Foreword
    Robert E. Rice x

Introduction 1
    Yolanda T. Capulong, Ed.D. xii

Introduction 2
    Henry Klopping, Ed.D. xiii

Acknowledgements xiv

Acronyms xvi

Quotation
    Delight Rice .... xvii (1)

1 Early Days of the Rice Family 2

2 Education: 1901-1907 12

3 Philippine Search: 1907 24

4 School for the Deaf and the Blind 34

    Ermita School: 1907-1908 36

    Intramuros School: 1908-1910 48

    Port District School: 1910-1923 52

    Pasay School: 1923-Present 68

5 California School for the Deaf 74

6 Rice Family: 1910-1923 86

7 Rice Family: 1923-1964 96

8 Centennial Celebration: 2007 116

    Delight Rice's Timeline 124

    About the Author
    Ronald M. Hirano 134

    Appendix
    Principals and Officers-in-Charge 138

    Maps 142

    Bibliography 148

    Index 160

Mission

Proceeds from the sale of this book will go toward a proposed sculpture of Delight Rice, Ped.D. This sculpture is to be erected on the campus of Philippine School for the Deaf in Pasay City.

Delight Rice was an extraordinary teacher and principal who was responsible for many unprecedented achievements in Deaf education. To perpetuate her legacy, the sculpture is in memoriam of Mother Delight Rice, who had a heart of gold. Contributions are greatly appreciated and will help her memory thrive for the Philippine School for the Deaf students, staffers, alumni, families and friends.

Preface

Ronald M. Hirano
Delight Rice's foster son
San Francisco, California

While growing up in Delight Rice's loving care in Berkeley, California, from 1942 to 1949, I was always in awe as I watched her sign fluently about her life in the United States and the Philippines. She accompanied the stories with old, yet interesting, photos from her albums.

On September 29, 1945, deaf American Edward Roger and his hearing Filipino wife, along with their two children, returned to California from the Philippines. During their short stay at Delight's residence, they told me about Philippine School for the Deaf and their terrifying experiences during the Japanese occupation.

In January 1958, Richard West, the president of the Philippine Association of the Deaf and also a School for the Deaf and Blind (SDB) alumnus, came over to visit Delight and her brother Percy, nephew Robert, foster son Bernardo Cuengco and me at her house for a few weeks. They shared many interesting stories about her life in the Philippines. Those stories fascinated me so much that I decided to write this book.

I spent five years researching this book at the Gallaudet University Library and Archives in Washington, D.C., and California School for the Deaf Historical Museum in Fremont. I also gathered documents from Ohio, Wisconsin and Philippine Schools for the Deaf, and from friends in the Philippines as well as the United States. Through my research, I learned that information in other writings was likely inaccurate.

For several years, this book project was delayed by the lack of original photos. In December 2009, Delight's nephew, Robert Rice, found many old pictures while cleaning his house out. They were shipped to me, and I excitedly unpacked the boxes. A gold mine of information! There were several photograph albums dating between 1903 and 1963, a thick scrapbook of Delight's 1961-1962 Philippine visit, papers, newspaper clippings and other documents. The project was revitalized.

Delight and her parents wrote articles for deaf American publications. Her achievements and lectures were featured in major newspapers across the United States and the Philippines.

Delight remains renowned and beloved in the deaf and hearing communities in the Philippines. She often considered deaf Filipino pupils her children, and the alumni to this day call her Mother Delight Rice.

Delight's major achievements include:
- Pioneering the teaching of deaf-blind students at Wisconsin and Ohio Schools for the Deaf from 1903 through 1907, teaching three of those students simultaneously by herself.
- Establishing the first deaf school in the Philippines in 1907. To further deaf students' education, she enrolled several deaf Filipino students at the California School for the Deaf (CSD) in Berkeley from 1909 through 1923. She also encouraged them to continue at Gallaudet College (now University).
- Inaugurating the first class for hard of hearing children at the Berkeley Public Schools in 1928, and being one of the first to test their hearing and speech.
- Devising a new audiological testing method in 1932, and receiving an official commendation from the audiometer inventor.
- Recommending that parents send their deaf children to CSD from 1932 through 1939. All but one successfully passed entrance exams for Gallaudet College and eventually became leaders in the deaf community and in deaf education.

The Life Story of Mother Delight Rice and Her Children

- Being hired, despite lacking a college degree, as an audiology instructor at the College (now University) of the Pacific. Several applicants had doctorates but were not selected.

This book offers you insights into Delight's remarkable career as a pioneer in deaf education. Hopefully, her extraordinary legacy will endure for generations.

Ronald Hirano and Delight Rice
in Berkeley, California, 1944

Foreword

Robert E. Rice
Delight Rice's nephew
Tacoma, Washington

Genealogies can be rather impersonal and difficult to read. The author, Ronald Hirano, has compiled a biography incorporating the history of Delia Delight Rice, her relatives and friends in a way that is both interesting and factual.

For the most part, *Tia Mia*, as Delight was called, raised Ronald. He was in a unique position to research the life story of a remarkable woman, largely from his contacts at Gallaudet University.

The story of Delight's life begins in central Ohio, where C. M. Rice and his wife lived. Delight was the oldest of their three children, which also included her brothers Percy and Freeman. Both parents were deaf. It was natural then that Delight became associated with the local deaf community and went on to be a teacher of the deaf and blind. In this book, Ronald has described her early education and traced her life throughout her subsequent career.

In short, Tia Mia lived a life of giving to others. Following the early death of her brother Percy's wife, she took on the task of raising her nephew Buddy as if he were her own, when he was just seven years of age.

During the Great Depression of the 1930s, she opened her home at 2149 Blake Street in Berkeley to her brothers and their families as a shelter from economic hardships. Her father lived there as well until his death. As the Depression wore on, there were nine family members living in the Blake Street home. Tia Mia, in addition to supporting her relatives, contributed to the education of more than a dozen young men, both relatives and non-relatives, including Bernardo Cuengco from the Philippines, Roy Saami, and of course Ronald and me.

Delight was a devoted Christian and took great pride in her family values. At the same time, she gave fully to others families and friends. On any given Sunday, she would be in the back row of the church, interpreting the sermon and proceedings for the benefit of any and all deaf and hard of hearing parishioners.

It is fitting that this book is written at this time since this "branch" of the Rice family will come to an end with my passing. Bud and I had seven children between us. None of our children have sons or daughters, so we represent the end of a long line of Rices stretching back to New England in the 1600s. On behalf of the Rice family, we thank Ronald for all the hard work that went into this biography.

Author's Note: *Robert Rice passed away on February 14, 2014.*

Robert Rice, Delight Rice and Ronald Hirano
in Berkeley, California, July 1943

Introduction 1

Yolanda T. Capulong, Ed.D.
Special Schools Principal II (1987-Present)
Philippine School for the Deaf
Pasay, Metro Manila, Philippines

Ronald Hirano's book takes stock of the life lived by Delight Rice as the pioneering educator of the deaf in the Philippines. It chronicles the journey of this wonderful lady to a place far from home to fulfill a noble and purposeful goal: to educate Filipino children who were disabled. While her work as principal of the school also included blind children, this book provides a rich visual representation of important facts about Delight's family, her initiatives in establishing an instructional system for a diverse group of Filipino deaf children, and what Philippine School for the Deaf is today — more than one hundred years after she initially set foot in the country.

This work serves as a legacy and invaluable source of information that will augment the scanty resources about this lady. Being the administrator of this national special school started by Delight, this book finally connects me to the past and rich heritage that I will pass on to future generations of deaf children and advocates of the Filipino deaf community. It is an honor to "meet" Delight through this work and to trace her footsteps in this place that I have been a part of since 1971.

Her life and works deserve to be known, given how she had a very profound impact on the education of students who have disabilities in the country. Whatever gains the Philippines have in deaf education started with a seed of love planted by Mother Delight Rice. It is perfectly right that she be immortalized through an accurate presentation of details that only Ronald can execute.

The Life Story of Mother Delight Rice and Her Children

Introduction 2

Henry Klopping, Ed.D.
Superintendent (1975-2011)
California School for the Deaf
Berkeley and Fremont, California

Ronald Hirano has clearly communicated the major role that California School for the Deaf has played in the lives of deaf children from the Philippines. For many years, deaf students attending Philippine School for the Deaf, established by Delight Rice, completed their education at California School for the Deaf in Berkeley. Delight Rice was deeply loved by deaf students and became known as Mother Delight Rice because of her overriding love for the children she served. She encouraged, and supported, many children to attend California School for the Deaf and then Gallaudet College.

Mother Delight Rice touched Ronald's life, and this book sheds light on the major roles she had in other Deaf children's lives. Chapter 5 clearly details the role that California School for the Deaf played in the lives of the Filipino children who were fortunate enough to attend the school. She significantly improved the lives of deaf children in the Philippines by ensuring that they had a basic education established before coming to California School for the Deaf. Once they arrived at the school, finishing touches were placed on the outstanding work she began in the Philippines.

Ronald is to be thanked for helping preserve this crucial part of Deaf history so that it may be passed onto future generations of Deaf people, especially in the Philippines.

Acknowledgements

I wish to express my heartfelt and sincere appreciation for all the support I received. Without the support, this book project would not be possible.

My special thanks go to **Alice Hagemeyer,** a Gallaudet University classmate who is also a prominent activist in library services for deaf people. She persistently encouraged me to write this book.

I am indebted to Delight Rice's nephew, **Robert Rice,** for his generous contribution of original photographs and documents. These materials helped my book project make a huge leap forward. I also extend my thanks to his friend, film producer **Candice Critchfield,** for getting information from the Library of Congress.

Information used in this writing of the book came from a multitude of individuals. From the bottom of my heart, I thank **Thomas Bull,** a retired Gallaudet University staff interpreter; the late **Frances Parsons,** a retired Gallaudet University professor; **Newby Ely,** a researcher on deaf Japanese-American internees; **Rodolfo Soriano** and **Renato Cruz,** Philippine School for the Deaf alumni; **Richard Hubner,** an Ohio School for the Deaf alumnus; **Milton and Joy Lee** and **Thomas Harbison,** alumni and retired teachers of the Wisconsin School for the Deaf; **Charo David,** a Philippine School for the Deaf teacher; **Millie Barnhart,** a researcher at the Delaware County Genealogical Society; and **Nancy Boone** and **Donna Henderson,** Ohio School for the Deaf librarians.

Gratitude for wonderful and valuable assistance in the preparation of this book goes to **Diana Moore,** a Gallaudet University librarian; **Michael Olson,** an archivist at the Gallaudet University Archives; **Melvin Pedersen,** a volunteer at the California School for the Deaf Historical Museum; **Orkideh Sassouni** and **Jerry Kapsner,** librarians at the Deaf Services of San Francisco Public Library; **Kenneth Norton,** a California School for the Deaf historian; **Robert Strohmeier,** a New Jersey School for the Deaf historian; **Joyce Ingraham,** a genealogist and proofreader; **Anita Ortiz Ner, Susana Vergara Cofer** and **Roy Luster,** Philippine School for the Deaf alumni; **Nanae and Lydia Ho, Joseph McLaughlin, Chuck Hom,** and **Stanley and Marie Smith,** friends; my sister **Carol Hirano;** and the staff of **T.S. Writing Services.**

Percy Rice, Delight Rice and Bernardo Cuengco
Brothers Robert and Ronald Hirano
in Berkeley, California, 1946

Acronyms

ASL	American Sign Language
BAADA	Bay Area Asian Deaf Association
BACDSC	Bay Area Coalition of Deaf Senior Citizens
BDA	Bohol Deaf Academy
BSA	Boy Scouts of America
CAD	California Association of the Deaf
CAID	Convention of American Instructors of the Deaf
CHS	Columbus High School
CNS	Columbus Normal School
CSD	California School for the Deaf
CSDAA	California School for the Deaf Alumni Association
CSDB	California School for the Deaf and Blind
DCARA	Deaf Counseling, Advocacy & Referral Agency
DSA	Deaf Seniors of America
EBCD	East Bay Club for the Deaf
FBI	Federal Bureau of Investigation
FSL	Filipino Sign Language
HCMLA	Hearing Center of Metropolitan Los Angeles
IDEA	International Deaf Education Association
NAD	National Association of the Deaf
NFSD	National Fraternal Society of the Deaf
OSD	Ohio School for the Deaf
OSDAA	Ohio School for the Deaf Alumni Association
PAD	Philippine Association of the Deaf
PNS	Philippine Normal School (now University)
PSD	Philippine School for the Deaf
SAID	Southeast Asia Institute for the Deaf
SDB	School for the Deaf and the Blind (now PSD)
SFCD	San Francisco Club for the Deaf
SFSU	San Francisco State University
SWCID	SouthWest Collegiate Institute for the Deaf
UC	University of California
USAT	United States Army Transport
WFD	World Federation of the Deaf
WSD	Wisconsin School for the Deaf

　　　　　　　The Life Story of Mother Delight Rice and Her Children

While the responsibility is great and the task at times almost overwhelming, the pupils never know it. They are encouraged to grow physically, mentally, morally; to look forward to the time when they will boldly compete in various walks of life with the hearing and sighted, with just as good and at times much better success than their more fortunate fellowmen.

— Delight Rice

Rice Family Gathering

**Early Days of
the Rice Family**

132 - 2
coded
√

no. 3114

[Please answer the questions as fully as possible, and return the record to E. A. Fay, Kendall Green, Washington, D. C.]

MARRIAGE RECORD

OF

Charles M. Rice (husband) and _Alice J. Gregg_ (wife)

1. DETAILS RELATING TO MARRIAGE.

1. _Date of Marriage?_ July 15. 1880. _Place of Marriage?_ Delaware, O.

Were the parties related before marriage? _____ _If so, what relationship?_ _____

Give any other details known relating to marriage. Married by

Supt. G. O. Fay.

2. OFFSPRING. _Total number of children born of this marriage?_ 3

How many were deaf? ____ _How many could hear?_ 3. _How many died in infancy?_ ____

Give any other details known relating to offspring. For example, names, dates of birth or death, causes of death, ages at death, etc., where possible.

George M. b. July 1. 1881. died Oct 12 '83 from poison.

Celia Delight - 3. 1883.

Percy Eugene - Feb. 21. 1888.

This marriage record was found in the _U.S. Special Census on Deaf Family, Marriage and Hearing Relatives, 1888-1895,_ the official supplement to the 1890 U.S. Census. It was promoted by the Volta Bureau, the national headquarters of Alexander Graham Bell Association for the Deaf. Dr. Edward Allen Fay, appointed by the government, collected and researched questionnaires at Gallaudet College.

Chapter 1

EARLY DAYS OF THE RICE FAMILY

Historical Fact: Ohio's Early Years

In the early nineteenth century, pioneers from the East Coast settled in the new state of Ohio, created out of the Northwest Territory in 1803. Named for explorer Christopher Columbus, the city and state capital of Columbus was founded in 1812.

Knox County was created on January 30, 1808, formed from Fairfield and Franklin Counties. Milford Township, established in Knox County in 1823, was forty-one miles northeast of Columbus. It was named after the oldest settler's native town of New Milford, Connecticut. Mount Liberty, an unincorporated community in Knox County, is ten miles southwest of county seat Mount Vernon.

Father: Charles Merrick Rice

Born in Mount Vernon on September 19, 1854, Charles Merrick Rice was the second of three children. He lost his hearing at the age of ten years as the result of illness. He became very skilled at speechreading. He graduated from Ohio School for the Deaf (OSD) in Columbus on June 16, 1874. That following fall, he enrolled at Gallaudet College (now University) in Washington, D.C., as a Class of 1879 member, and stayed for four years. Due to financial difficulties, he did not graduate.

Charles Merrick Rice

Charles' parents were James Chandler Rice (1815-1858) of Massachusetts and Martha Ann Hawkins (1823?-1892) of Knox County. They were married in Knox County on June 18, 1848. For several years, he was a postmaster at a post office called Milfordton established in 1843. Martha's parents, Harris Hawkins (1787-1856) and Phebe Lowell (1791-1841), both came from Rhode Island. He was the township's first blacksmith.

Mother: Alice Isadora Gregg

Born in Delaware, Ohio, on July 10, 1858, Alice Isadora Gregg was the oldest of two girls born to John Gregg (1810?-1880) of Indiana and Cecelia Delight Alexander (1834-1896) of Ohio. Alice lost her hearing at fourteen years of age due to illness. Like Charles, she became an excellent speechreader. She is believed to have graduated from OSD in 1879.

Alice Isadora Rice

Alice's parents were married on May 21, 1854, in Jonesboro, Indiana. They were divorced in Delaware in November 1864 as a result of his adultery with at least three women.

Alice's sister Delia married John Schaller in 1883. When she was twenty-eight, he slit her throat in Cincinnati out of insane jealousy. The murder-suicide left their daughters Mary and Agnes (known as "Kittie") orphans; their grandmother Cecelia legally adopted them.

Cecelia was the daughter of Joseph C. Alexander (1808-1889) of Pennsylvania and Delight P. Sweetser (1803-1866) of Vermont. He and Delight were married on September 22, 1833, and settled on a farm in Delaware. He was a Union Civil War soldier with Company K, 66th Regiment, Ohio Infantry. The Alexander family members are buried in the Oak Grove Cemetery in Delaware.

Rice Family

On July 15, 1880, OSD Superintendent Gilbert Otis Fay performed the marriage of Charles and Alice under a tree at Cecelia's residence in Delaware. The Rices had four hearing children: George Merrick Rice (1881-1883, of poisoning), Delia Delight Rice (1883-1964), Percy Eugene Rice (1888-1959) and Charles Freeman Rice (1896-1957). The elder Charles was employed as a plasterer at

Delight and Percy Rice

Baby Freeman, Percy and Delight Rice

a shop in Columbus, and at another time, at OSD in 1906 or 1907, and then as a clerk with the Ohio State Insurance Board.

Delia Delight Rice

Born on a farm in Milfordton (or Milford) on July 3, 1883, Delia Delight Rice was named after her aunt Delia Gregg and her grandmother Cecelia Delight Alexander.

When Delight was three, the family moved to Columbus. As a child, she often spent summers with her grandmother Martha in Milfordton.

Brother: Percy Eugene Rice

Percy Eugene Rice was employed as a clerk for the Pennsylvania Railroad while living with his parents in Columbus. During the World War One, he tried to enlist in the U.S. Army, but failed the exam. The Alaska Territory beckoned him to become a sampler/miner for the Juneau Gold Mining Company in Juneau. In June 1917, he and Ester Louella Sutten, born in 1898 in Iowa, were married in Juneau. They later moved to Seattle, Washington, where he landed a job as a checker at a flour mill. Their first-born, Charles "Buddy" Sutton Rice, arrived on October 13, 1918. When Percy was widowed in 1926, his sister Delight became a guardian of seven-year-old Buddy.

Percy Eugene Rice

Three years later, Percy married Leda Rosemond Fife (1909-1981) in Seattle, where he was employed as a bookkeeper for a brick factory. Leda birthed Robert Eugene Rice on August 8, 1930. After they divorced in 1939 or 1940, Percy resided with Delight in Berkeley and in 1945, Robert went to live with them in order to attend a better high school. He always called Delight *Tia Mia*, Spanish for "my aunt."

Percy worked as a stamping machine operator at Marchant Calculating Machine Company in Oakland. Later, he was employed at Cutter Laboratories in Berkeley. On April 1, 1959, he passed away at a rest home in Oakland, and was buried in the Rice family plot at the Five Corners Cemetery in Milfordton.

Brother: Charles Freeman Rice

Charles Freeman Rice followed his family to Manila, Philippines, in 1910, where he resided with his parents and sister Delight while working as an officer for area newspapers. In September 1912, he was appointed as a supervisor for blind boys at California School for the Deaf (CSD) and Blind (CSDB) in Berkeley. In June 1914, he resigned from that position and enrolled at Gallaudet College as a normal student in the Class of 1915.

Charles Freeman Rice

The following year he left Gallaudet and returned to Berkeley where his mother lived, working at the Sunset Lumber Company in nearby Oakland. In 1917, he worked for the Treadwell Mining Company at a gold mine in Alaska for two years. After the war, he worked in real estate in Los Angeles until he started volunteering for the U.S. Navy. He was trained as a second-class yeoman for the U.S. Navy Submarine Chaser in San Pedro for six months. He and his crew sailed for Pago Pago, American Samoa, and returned to San Francisco in August 1919. He was promoted to the rank of lieutenant or captain.

In 1922-1923, he played for the CSD football team, the Foothills. In 1924, he wrote for the *San Luis Obispo Herald* newspaper. He also served as a scoutmaster of Boy Scouts of America (BSA) Troop 11 at CSD a few years later, and was a cigar industry representative in Los Angeles in the late 1920s and 1930s. In the 1940s, he owned a hearing aid business in downtown Oakland.

Charles was married several times, but had no children. He was buried at the Golden Gate National Cemetery in San Bruno.

Nephew: Charles "Buddy" Sutton Rice

Charles "Buddy" Sutton Rice enlisted as an Army Air Corps aviation cadet at the Presidio of San Francisco shortly after graduation from the University of California in 1940.

During peacetime, military bases were operated five days a week, and everybody, including commanders, had Saturdays and Sundays off. The individual appointed as officer of the day had to sit in the main office in case of an emergency.

At Wheeler Army Airfield in Oahu, Hawaii, Buddy was appointed officer of the day on Sunday, December 7, 1941. On that fateful day, the base was the first target of the Pearl Harbor bombing. As a second lieutenant, just six months out of flying school, Buddy and his squadron flew Douglas A-20 Havoc twin-engined light attack bombers for the first half of the war and then Douglas A-26 Invaders. He served the entire war in the Pacific theater right up to the end of the invasion of Okinawa. In 1945, he came home as a captain and senior pilot after logging more than three thousand flying hours.

Charles "Buddy" Sutton Rice

In 1941, Buddy married Sarah Yvonne West in Palo Alto, California. Born February 1, 1918, in San Francisco, Yvonne graduated from Galileo High School in 1934, and from Fresno State College (now University) in 1939. Their union produced four children: Charles "Beau" Beauregard, born 1944 in South Carolina; Jane, born 1947 in Ohio; Anne, born 1949 in Sweden; and Robert "Bobby" Sutton, born 1953 in Virginia after the family moved back to the U.S. from Europe. In 1973, Yvonne passed away. Buddy later married Mary Eidd Hallow (1924-2005), the daughter of Syrian immigrants and an accountant with the Civil Service at Langley Air Force Base in Langley, Virginia.

Buddy passed away on July 7, 1994, in Morehead City, North Carolina, and was buried in Goldsboro, North Carolina.

Nephew: Robert Eugene Rice

Robert Eugene Rice attended the University of California. The Korean War was underway so it was possible he would be drafted. He received a deferment in 1950 to finish college. Upon graduation in June 1952, he was sent to Korea to serve the U.S. Air Force as a Second Lieutenant in the 15th Tactical Reconnaissance Squadron. The squadron was transferred from Korea to Japan where he flew the RF-80, the RF-84F and RF-86F until 1956. After an honorable discharge from military service in 1956, he started a forestry career as a pre-cutting tree inspector for U.S. Plywood in Redding, California, where he remained until 1969. He moved to Tacoma, Washington, to become a timber sales manager at Weyerhauser Company, which included four years in Hong Kong as a sales manager and shipping coordinator. He took early retirement from Weyerhauser Company in 1985. From 1985 to 1998, he was vice president of Citifor, a Chinese-based company, before he retired again.

Robert Eugene Rice

After meeting as students at Berkeley High School, Robert and Marie Bauer married December 20, 1953, in Berkeley. Born to immigrant parents in San Francisco on January 26, 1932, Marie graduated from the University of California with a history degree in 1953. She and Robert raised three daughters: Jeanine Marie Delight, born in 1955; Julianne Elaine, born in 1959; and Joan Willette, born in 1961. Marie was an English teacher at a Chinese middle school in Hong Kong. When she and Robert returned to Tacoma, she taught English as a second language to new immigrants for twelve years. She was an amateur genealogist and authored three books on the Longmire, Hansen and Marini families. She passed away on July 4, 2011.

Robert Rice, the last surviving nephew of Delight Rice, passed away on February 14, 2014.

Charles "Buddy" Rice, Delight Rice and Robert Rice

Wisconsin School
for the Deaf
1903-1904

Delight
Rice ◢

Education
1901-1907

Chapter **2**

Delight
Rice

Dr. Edward Miner
Gallaudet,
First President of
Gallaudet College
▼

Convention of American Instructors for the Deaf
July 8-15, 1905

North Carolina School for the Deaf
Morganton, North Carolina

Chapter 2

EDUCATION 1901-1907

Although there is a minimal information on Delight's early schooling years, research indicates that she was well-educated.

Central High School

Central High School (CHS), one of the first six high schools in Columbus, was located downtown from 1862 until 1924. Delight graduated from CHS in 1901. When Gallaudet College opened up its Normal School, later the Graduate School, she applied for admission in May 1901. Her application, for unknown reasons, was not accepted.

Columbus Normal School

In September 1901, Delight enrolled at the Columbus Normal School (CNS). As a CNS student, she supervised playgrounds during summer breaks. In recommending her for a position as a teacher at a school, the CNS principal wrote:

She has given us great satisfaction as both a pupil and a teacher. Her work is carefully prepared, skillfully taught, and her management of a class is very good.

Delight graduated with a teacher's certificate from CNS in February 1903.

Ohio School for the Deaf

In 1829, Ohio Institution for the Education of the Deaf and Dumb (now Ohio School for the Deaf, or OSD) was established near the State Legislature in Columbus. In 1953, it was relocated to the present site on 235 acres with a creek on the far north side of the city. The construction of school buildings was patterned after CSD in Berkeley.

Ohio School for the Deaf in Columbus
Established in 1829

In addition to her existing qualifications, Delight was trained for oral education by her supervisor of speech at OSD. Subsequently, she served as a substitute teacher at different schools in Columbus for some time.

OSD Alumni Association and Columbus Colony

In 1870, Ohio Deaf-Mute Alumni Association (now Ohio School for the Deaf Alumni Association, or OSDAA) was established in Columbus. It is today the oldest alumni association of any kind in the nation. In 1896, OSDAA opened the first retirement facility in the nation for deaf people, Ohio Home for the Aged and Infirm Deaf (now Columbus Colony) in Westerville. Under OSDAA's current management, Columbus Colony is one of the nation's most prestigious retirement complexes for deaf residents.

OSDAA members considered Delight unsurpassed as an expert interpreter in sign language among her colleagues. She was appointed as an honorary OSDAA member at its eleventh reunion in Columbus in 1901.

Wisconsin School for the Deaf

Founded in 1852, Wisconsin School for the Deaf, or WSD, is located in the small rural town of Delavan with a population of approximately eight thousand people, fifty-four miles southwest of Milwaukee. Delavan was home to twenty-six circus companies between 1847 and 1894.

In September 1903, Delight was one of two OSD instructors who transferred to WSD and became a special teacher of deaf-blind students.

Delight's Trio

Delight was in the midst of some of the most interesting work performed by a young woman in those days, certainly a most arduous task. She taught three deaf-blind girls, called "Wisconsin's Helen Kellers," simultaneously at a time when the policy was one student per teacher. Each girl was eighteen years old, and Delight was twenty-two. In the entire country, there were only about thirty deaf-blind students. Here was a bright and faithful young worker who had undertaken educating one-tenth of the nation's deaf-blind population, and her success was nothing short of marvelous.

Delight was splendidly fitted for her work in both temperament and education. She was a master of sign language and, as an interpreter, was among the very best in her skills. The students were very intelligent and learned quickly, almost entirely via tactile methods. Delight made every possible effort to develop the girls' articulation.

Eva Halliday

Born near Wausau, Wisconsin, in 1887, Eva Halliday became deaf from an illness at age five and, a year later, lost her sight from the same illness. At fifteen, she entered WSD. She learned to read and to rapidly operate Braille and Remington typewriters. She was also taught speech by placing her fingers upon the speaker's lips. During her two years at

Wisconsin School for the Deaf in Delavan
Established in 1852

Anna Johnson, Delight Rice, Minnie Dunick and Eva Halliday
Wisconsin's "Helen Kellers"

WSD, Eva made more progress than any other deaf-blind student in the nation, including Helen Keller. She was attractive, bright and ambitious, and became a favorite among teachers and pupils.

Delight took Eva with her to the fifty-second annual convention of the Wisconsin Teachers' Association in Milwaukee on December 27-30, 1904. It was the largest and most interesting gathering of educators ever held in the state, with more than three thousand people. The first feature of the program was a demonstration by Eva, much to the participants' surprise.

Anna Johnson

Born near Colfax, Wisconsin, in 1887, Anna Johnson was a bright and ambitious country school girl who lost her sight and hearing at the age of twelve years. She went to WSD in January 1904, and had a vocabulary and speaking skills developed prior to her sight and hearing loss. She could distinguish light and shadowy forms. The challenge in teaching her was quite different from that of teaching Eva; Anna had only to master the point system used by blind people and learn the manipulation of typewriters. She achieved much in the short time she was at WSD. She spoke well and had a pleasant voice, according to the April 4, 1904, issue of the *Wisconsin Times*.

Both Eva and Anna were happy, light-hearted girls. They were optimistic and thoroughly appreciative of all done for them. Delight was constantly finding new ways to educate them. During the summer of 1904, she took Eva and Anna to the St. Louis International Exposition where little by little, she conveyed what was taking place.

Minnie Dunick

Born in Milwaukee in 1887, Minnie Dunick lost her sight and hearing at age twelve, like Anna. She could see in a very limited sense, though nothing distinctly. She came to WSD in the fall of 1904. Her speech was good, but her voice was weak.

A visit to the school was never complete without a call on these three girls.

Teaching Method

Delight employed a largely tactile approach, especially in feeling objects, in her education. To teach the word "ditch," she took Eva to a nearby highway where a large excavation took place. The two clambered down to the bottom of the ditch, where Eva felt the sides and bottom, the height and width, and the earth and rock formation. As Eva touched each item, Delight fingerspelled into Eva's hand the words for each. To teach her students about the American flag, she taught them to find, via touch, the locality of stars and stripes, and even the stripes' alternating colors, the field's color, and the stars' shapes. To ensure understanding of a star, the students learned how to form a star out of sand. These students went to many meetings and conventions to display their accomplishments.

Delight Rice

Wisconsin School for the Deaf Staff
at Delavan Lake in 1903

Presentation at the Convention

On July 12, 1905, Delight presented *The Importance of Teaching the Blind-Deaf to Work* at the Seventeenth Triennial Convention of the American Instructors of the Deaf (CAID), held at the North Carolina School for the Deaf in Morganton. Much to the audience's fascination, she read her entire script in sign language, with WSD Supt. E.W. Walker voicing for her.

Below are excerpts from her presentation.

> *In the care and education of persons not blessed with the faculties of hearing and seeing, happiness and contentment should be the primary and most important condition sought for. The first step in this direction is the creating or kindling of the spark of ambition. The mind must feel that this dual affliction has not placed it beyond the pale of usefulness and service. Individual instruction is necessary as a beginning, for the unimpaired senses must be cultivated to perform the functions of those destroyed through disease or accident.*

Fortified with developed minds, they will meet the problems of life and be better prepared to cope with them. The nearer they approach the intellectual equality of their fellow-beings, the more their sense of isolation will diminish. The real essence of philanthropy consists in helping man to help himself. The opening of some avenue for growth and expansion will prevent the unprofitable and harmful musings of idleness. The sense of touch can be utilized for everything, but the distinguishing of color; even this is not impossible.

Lessons in manual training may develop a taste for architecture or sculpture. Massaging, also, is quite practical. The blind of Japan are especially most proficient in this art and achieve most satisfactory results. Deafness need not be regarded as an impediment. Bookbinding, copying for the blind, and sewing are excellent. Doll's clothing and embroidering are possible. In competitive exhibitions, the specimens displayed by blind-deaf girls have often been approved over those submitted by pupils who have the use of all their faculties. Their opportunities are as many and occur in any work undertaken. For the blind-deaf, wholesome literature and work, steady work, led to happiness with an education as the only means.

The entire presentation was featured in the July 13, 1905 issue of the *Charlotte Daily Observer* as well as being the cover story in the October 14, 1905 issue of WSD's *Wisconsin Times*.

Return to Ohio

In May 1906, Delight resigned from WSD to return to Columbus so she could teach at OSD. That fall, she was assigned to work as a special teacher of two deaf-blind boys, John Porter Ripley (a black student), and Wilbur Reynolds. Wilbur had been refused admission to various schools throughout the state, ultimately ending up at OSD. She made extraordinary progress with John, but soon discovered that Wilbur could hear. Upon her report, the superintendent dismissed him. The efforts to get him into other state institutions were fully covered by local newspapers.

U.S. Civil Service Examination

In the December 15, 1906, issue of the OSD periodical *Ohio Chronicle,* a circular from the U.S. Civil Service Commission announced an examination for the position of a teacher of the deaf in Philippine Islands. The examination was to be held in Columbus and other cities in Ohio. The appointed teacher was expected to arrive in Manila at the beginning of the school year on June 9, 1907.

On January 25, 1907, Delight took the examination and was the only one who passed. She was given a three-year contract at a thousand dollars per year. She received a telegram from the Insular Bureau asking if she could sail for the Philippines on April 23 or May 3, 1907.

The *Columbus Dispatch* stated in a Sunday edition:

> *Delight Rice, however, is highly ambitious, and in the new field will be given opportunities to show her abilities. It is a new departure of the U.S. government and it is her understanding that when she reaches the Philippines she will be given full sway, and be allowed to put in practice many of the theories that her experience has developed.*

Edward Miner Gallaudet, Ed.D., the first president of Gallaudet College, corresponded with Delight and took a personal interest in her as his favorite "daughter." He, as did several others, encouraged her to establish a deaf school in the Philippines.

More accustomed to deaf students than blind students, Delight chose to start a class dedicated to deaf students.

Delight Rice and Eva Halliday
at Wisconsin School for the Deaf in 1904

American
Constabularies
and Delight Rice

Chapter **3**

Philippine
Search
1907

Igorot
Headhunter

Chapter 3

PHILIPPINE SEARCH 1907

Historical Fact: The Philippine Islands

Portuguese explorer Ferdinand Magellan and his Spanish expedition discovered the Philippines on March 16, 1521. The Spanish colonization and settlement began with the arrival of Spanish conquistador Miguel López de Legazi's expedition on February 13, 1565. In 1571, de Legazi founded the fortified city of Manila (now Intramuros). During the Spanish-American War of 1898, American military forces occupied the Philippines, ending 333 years of the Spanish colonial rule. After the end of the American rule in 1941 and the Japanese military occupation of 1941-1945, the Philippines finally became an independent republic in 1946.

Thomasites and Peace Corps

On August 23, 1901, the pioneering five hundred American teachers known as Thomasites left from San Francisco and reached Manila aboard the U.S. Army Transport (USAT) *Thomas*, formerly the Atlantic Transport Line ship *SS Minnewaska*. In the takeover from the U.S. Army, the Thomasites established a new public school system to provide basic education and to train Filipino teachers using English as the language of instruction. Schools and college buildings were built.

In 1961, President John F. Kennedy established a new American volunteer program, the Peace Corps, following the tradition initiated by the Thomasites. A good number of Peace Corps volunteers were deaf, such as Frances Parsons of Gallaudet University. She later trained volunteers at the Southeast Asia Institute for the Deaf (SAID), established in 1974 and located on the Miriam College campus in Quezon City, Manila. From 1976 to 1981, sixteen Peace Corps volunteers were trained for teaching duties at SAID. The school has sent numerous graduates to Gallaudet University and Miriam College.

U.S. Army Transport *Thomas*

In 1985, Peace Corps volunteers Dennis Drake and John Fisher started a deaf education program called International Deaf Education Association (IDEA) in Tagbilaran City, Bohol Island in the southern part of the Philippines. The IDEA today trains students and employs graduates to run business at the Dao Diamond Hotel, the Garden Cafe, and the SureCatch Fishing Products that sell feathered fishing hooks to sporting goods shops in Montana. A deaf construction crew built Bohol Deaf Academy (BDA) in 2005 and later renovated a home for deaf children in Maasin City, Southern Leyte Island.

Dr. David P. Barrows

David P. Barrows, Ed.D., a professor at University of California in Berkeley, served on the State Board of Control of California, the entity responsible for overseeing CSDB. In 1903, U.S. President Theodore Roosevelt appointed him as the Director of Bureau of Education of the Philippines. Based on the most recent Philippines census, ninety-two deaf individuals were identified in Manila and thousands more in the provinces. Barrows used that to plan on their education. He later became the president of University of California in Berkeley (1919-1923).

Delight's Arrival in Manila

On May 3, 1907, Delight departed San Francisco aboard the *USAT Thomas* and arrived in Manila on June 9, 1907. Among her personal papers was this account:

> *Many American teachers immediately called upon me. They were astounded that Dr. Barrows should go to the expense of sending a special teacher when they had never seen a deaf child in all the islands. They said there were a few blind adults and probably some blind children, but not enough for the opening of a special school.*

The local papers called it amusing and ridiculous to send a teacher so far. There were headlines asking, "Where are Miss Delight Rice's Children?" The Bureau of Education asked the Bureau of Health to conduct a special census, which failed to find a single deaf child.

Gilbert Brink had worked as a supervisor for boys at CSDB from September 1898 until March 1900, before becoming assistant director of the Bureau of Education in the Philippines. Upon Delight's arrival, he assigned a room to her at the Philippine Normal School (PNS) on Calle Padre Faura. Newspapers discussed how she often roamed the grounds all day while waiting for her duties. She occasionally went shopping or out with friends.

Manila Bay

Search for Deaf Children

Delight ventured into provinces around Manila seeking deaf children. They were rarely seen in public, as she wrote:

> *Eventually, we came to the question of deaf children. They were called* desgraciadas *(unfortunates) and the common belief was that they were sent as a direct punishment from God to the parents for misconduct. For this reason, deafness was concealed. Children with this handicap herded* carabaos *(water buffalos), carried water, and helped with the house work. They never appeared before strangers. This shame was the reason that no Americans knew of the existence of deaf children.*

The parents were suspicious of Delight's mission, and rumors about her began to spread. One was she intended to take deaf children to the United States where their heads would be chopped off, turned into golden *carabaos,* and sold out to amass her personal wealth.

Delight Rice Seeking Deaf Children
at nipa huts, also known as *bahay kubo*

American Constabulary and Delight Rice
in front of a U.S. Army wagon

Paula Felizardo

The highly publicized newspaper stories attracted the attention of a hearing child who thought he saw a deaf child in a house's laundry room. Delight accompanied him there and found a five-year-old girl. At first, an old man in the house denied the child's existence, but finally admitted that he was the child's father and that she was, indeed, deaf. Delight asked him to let her have the child and in turn, she would hire him to be her laundryman. He quickly agreed, making Paula Felizardo Delight's first pupil. She was not only pretty, but also bright. She quickly learned the word "sky" and "the sky is blue," and began to recognize her name and learn the names for objects.

Sergio Papa

After the publicity reached a town in Albay Province in southern Luzon, a family brought fifteen-year-old Sergio Papa to Manila to see Delight. After a few years under her tuition, he was sent to the Philippine Trade School for instruction in carpentry. He was Delight's first student who successfully made a living and returned home to his grateful family.

Delight Rice Seeking Deaf Children
at a nipa hut in a tribal village (*barangay*)

Pedro Santos

During the many hours and even days of Delight's search, a very few parents consented to sending their children to Manila for education. She once went to a largely Protestant town. Her interpreter asked the father of a deaf boy if he would like to send the boy to Manila. The father quickly responded in English, "Why not?" That child was Pedro Santos.

Search for Deaf Children

The Bureau of Education obtained permission from the Bureau of Health and Constabulary for Delight to travel through nearby provinces with student Paula Felizardo, so Paula could demonstrate what she had learned. Armed escorts were provided because of the lurking dangers of wild, hostile tribes inhabiting the remote provinces. The duo had receptions at local Filipino homes and stayed with American teachers at U.S. Army posts. Accompanied by American constabularies, Delight rode horses and burros for 1,000 to 1,500 miles throughout the mountainous landscape. She wore a bracelet, presented to her by a Moro, for protection. This was remarkable because no other white woman had the courage to approach the ferocious Moros. Delight gathered more information from the Moros through gestures rather than via her interpreter.

It took three months for Delight to find the first deaf child, although she brought at least one deaf pupil along on her travels so that she could demonstrate this deaf pupil's achievements to local natives. She slowly rounded up twenty-two, despite the belief that there were thousands in these areas. Her class grew so large that the establishment of a school became a necessity.

Early Beginnings of Deaf Education in the Philippines

Although Delight had identified twenty-two pupils, she conducted experimental work in teaching only four deaf pupils. The government supported her work at PNS, but did not offer provisions for the pupils. Two girls stayed in the school dormitory and two boys in a Catholic dormitory.

Poor parents in adjacent provinces could not afford to send their deaf children to Manila, so the school authorities obtained government funding to pay for expenses up to twenty pesos or ten U.S. dollars per month. A home in Manila provided lodging for twenty children; eleven children were sent there.

Delight Rice with American Constabularies

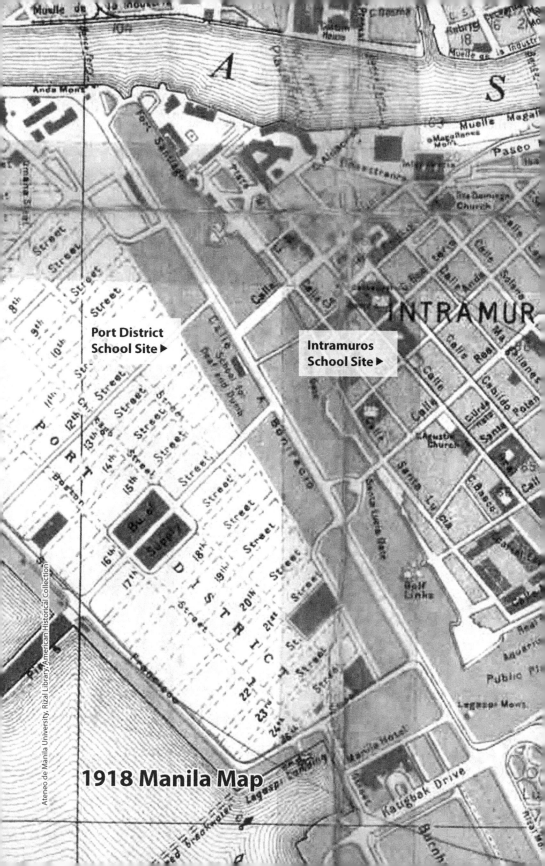

Port District
School Site ▶

Intramuros
School Site ▶

INTRAMUR

1918 Manila Map

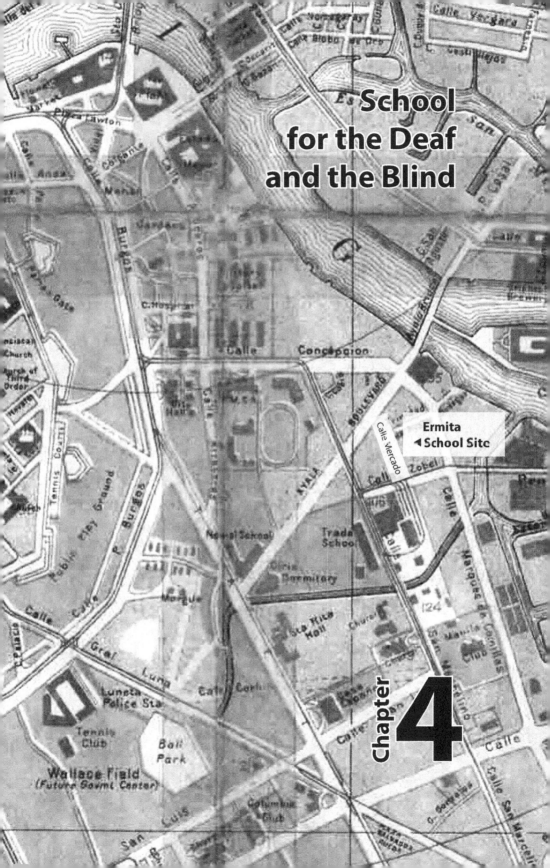

School
for the Deaf
and the Blind

Ermita
◀ School Site

Chapter 4

**Ermita School
on Calle Mercado**

Ermita School
1907-1908

Delight Rice
in front of
Ermita School

Chapter 4

SCHOOL FOR THE DEAF AND THE BLIND

Historical Fact: Ermita, District of Manila

Founded in the late sixteenth century, Ermita became a university district during the American rule and was largely populated by Americans. It now contains University of the Philippines, Philippine Normal University, and Ateneo de Manila University.

Ermita School 1907-1908

In 1907, Delight founded Manila Institute for the Deaf and Dumb (later renamed School for the Deaf and the Blind or SDB). The first class began with three pupils — two deaf and one blind — at a rented seven-room house in Ermita. Partitions were added to provide dormitories,

Delight Rice's First School Group
Back row: Delight Rice (far left), Paula Felizardo (in dark skirt), Rogerio Lagman (center) and Francisca Lagman (far right)

a dining room, a classroom and Delight's living quarters. The school was located on Calle Mercado, opposite the dormitory for PNS female students. The oldest student was eighteen years old and six feet tall while the youngest was a five-year-old chubby boy.

Rogerio and Francisca Lagman

Delight preferred to focus on her deaf students first, even though she had a blind student. She once visited a school in the town of Mexico, Pampanga Province, where a blind Filipino taught. That ambitious, studious young man, Rogerio Lagman, learned English from American soldiers. His faithful sister Francisca waited upon him, guided him and explained everything she saw. She followed him around, wrote on the blackboard, and read the lessons, practically serving as her brother's eyes. Rogerio passed all the primary and intermediate grades at the newly established public school system in Mexico. He was appointed as a teacher, and taught for several years before Delight's visit. In 1908, Rogerio was the first blind student in Delight's class, and Francisca became her first assistant.

Delight Rice Teaching Deaf Students at Ermita School

The Life Story of Mother Delight Rice and Her Children

Single Classroom in Ermita School

The sole blind student caused Dr. Barrows to consider opening a new blind school, but the school continued to serve both deaf and blind students.

Start of Second Term

When the second term began in July, there were thirteen pupils, with nine additional students later in the year. While the older boys began dropping out, more younger students were enrolling. As parents no longer had any more fear, they were more willing to send their children to the school.

Delight worked as principal, teacher, matron, mother, nurse, steward, cook and even dishwasher. When cholera became widespread, she labored to keep the school as sanitary as possible, even firing a cook for unsanitary practices and taking over cooking duties temporarily.

Religions

American soldiers and teachers took Delight's students to churches in the religions they practiced, usually Catholic and Protestant.

An American Protestant missionary from China visited the school and asked Delight about how many Christians enrolled. She answered that some students were Catholics, others Protestants, one Muslim and one was Jewish. The missionary replied, "I thought all Filipinos were Catholics." All the children received religious instruction according to their faiths.

School Amenities and Native Customs

In the school's early days, parents were allowed to stay overnight if they traveled from great distances and/or did not have sufficient money. This gave them the opportunity to observe how well their children were cared for. After the school became thoroughly established, the parents were no longer allowed to lodge there. However, many parents asked to stay again because the school had beds without any bedbugs.

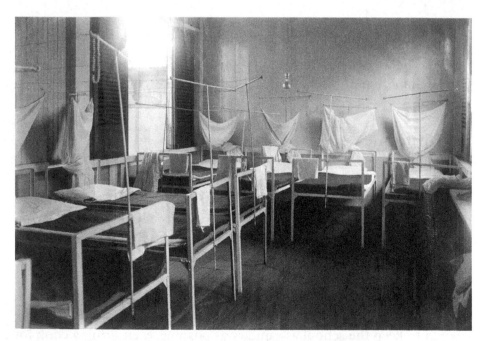

Student Dormitory in Ermita School

The Life Story of Mother Delight Rice and Her Children

Students Preparing to Bathe
Delight Rice (far left) and Francisca Lagman (far right)

Many children enrolled not knowing their birthdates, and a few of them did not have surnames. As a result, these children were given the choice of having national patriot Jose Rizal's (June 19) or Delight's birthday (July 3) as their birthdays. Rice was used for their surnames. When the boys reached the age of eighteen, they received *cedulas,* or certifications, for employment at the school.

The use of soap was unknown among Filipinos until the Americans came. Filipinos customarily kept themselves dirt-clean, as Delight often said. On Mondays, the girls returned to school with hair full with lice so she had to wash their hair thoroughly before classes began. On Tuesday nights, all older pupils took a shower while she scrubbed little ones in a hot bathtub. Over the first year, the children gradually learned to independently keep themselves clean.

Each student was provided a bed consisting of a mat, a single sheet, a pillow and a mosquito net covering. For protection from the cholera

Students in a Classroom
Front row: Delight Rice (far left) and Francisca Lagman (far right)
Middle row: Rogerio Lagman (far right)

epidemic, the Bureau of Health required all yards dusted with lime and all wooden toilets sprinkled with carbolic acid also known as phenol. The school's outdoor toilet consisted of a wooden bench with sitting holes, wooden pails and a shovel. Delight required much attention to its sanitation and taught her children how to use it properly like the Americans did. However, the neighbors began to use it and left it filthy. Despite Delight's insistence that it be cleaned and sprinkled again with the acid, the neighbors disliked the pungent odor and occasionally threw bucketfuls of water over the toilet.

Parents chatting with their deaf children often referred to Delight by pointing their index finger along the ridge of their nose. Sensitive about their flat noses, Filipinos always noticed Delight's Caucasian nose. One morning a little deaf girl showed up for breakfast with a very red, swollen nose. Delight was startled and wondered if it might be a disease. Upon further investigation, she discovered that the girl pinched her nose with her fingers and tried to use a clothespin to squeeze it into a shape similar to Delight's nose.

Offers from China

The Chinese Imperial government made several flattering teaching offers to Delight, but she rejected them all because of her contract with the United States government. She also felt she would have more opportunities for advancement by working for Uncle Sam.

Remarkable Encounters

One day Delight noticed one of her pupils missing. She learned of a gruesome discovery when the American authorities reported that the eight-year-old deaf-blind boy had been made a human sacrifice. Apparently, two widows asked their tribal headman, Datto Ansig, to appease the troubling ghosts of their husbands. He then conferred with

Upper Hallway of Ermita School

a council of elders and received approval. The custom was to sacrifice a slave, but as a result of a severe drought, the boy was selected because of his "infirmities."

Three days later, a group of villagers gathered for an elaborate ceremony by the riverbank. Ansig gave an oration:

Oh, Mandarangan, chief of evil spirits, and all the others spirits, come to our feast and accept our sacrifice. Let the sacrifice appease your wrath and take from us our misfortune, granting better times.

The boy was tied to a tree and killed by a spear thrust by those widows. His body was afterward cut into pieces. The authorities investigated that case. Ansig stated that he attended fifty human sacrifices, considered the victims of no use for the community, and could not understand why the authorities objected to the custom. "Can't you sacrifice an animal?" he was asked.

Delight Rice Outside Ermita School
Background: Dormitory for female students of Philippine Normal School

The Life Story of Mother Delight Rice and Her Children

Delight Rice at Ermita School

"No, better no sacrifice at all," he replied.

The authorities believed that it was a case for education rather than for punishment. But, to impress the lesson on the villagers, Datto Ansig and those widows were put on trial. The court announced that, according to new standards, human sacrifice was regarded as inhumane and intolerable. The offenders were sentenced to prison, but the sentence was suspended as long as there was no repetition of the act. This seemed to satisfy the general public, and the tribesmen swore never to offend again.

Intramuros School
on Calle Real
del Palacio

Intramuros
School
1908-1910

Historical Fact: Intramuros, District of Manila

Miguel López de Legazi founded the capital of Manila on June 24, 1571. He became the first governor-general and built forts, roads, churches and schools.

Completed in 1606, Intramuros was called the Walled City, surrounded by enormously thick, high fortress walls and wide moats. During the American rule, the moats were drained and filled. A few Americans resided there. It is today the oldest district of Manila.

Intramuros School 1908-1910

In 1908, SDB outgrew its quarters. A new building on Calle Real del Palacio (now General Luna Street) was built, completed and rented for school use by the government.

Delight appointed Paula Pecson, a hearing native PNS graduate, as an industrial teacher. This was welcome since Delight was burdened with teaching all classes and, in fact, the school's entire management. The children worshipped her and were ever ready to obey her. She attempted

Bridal Path along Malecon Street (later Calle A. Bonifacio)
Intramuro, left, and Port District School, right, several blocks away

to confine her pupils strictly to learning spelling and writing, but once they broke into signs, it was difficult to restrain their conversations.

Educational Methods

Delight used a combined method, adapted from OSD and Philippine public schools, consisting of reading, writing, fingerspelling, and speech to teach English. The oral (spoken) method was used only if it was actually beneficial.

The SDB provided calisthenics, folk dances and various games. Its literary club held biweekly exercises such as debates, reading and declamations.

The school subscribed to all magazines for deaf people and blind people. They helped pupils improve in reading and world knowledge. Delight regularly received *The Ohio Chronicle* from OSD by mail. When the mail came, her little children got excited. One boy called it "the paper with deaf pictures."

Manila Cathedral
One block from the Intramuros School site

Superstitious Parents

The school needed money as well as the parents' confidence. The natives were very superstitious, and they said they heard the children were to be taken to America and sold. It was an easy task to teach the child, but it was an impossibility to educate the parents.

Delight Rice and Francisca Lagman

Port District School on Malecon Drive

Port District School
1910-1923

Front Entrance of Port District School

Historical Fact: Port District, Manila

The Port of Manila and the surrounding area date back to the Spanish and pre-Spanish rule of the Philippine Islands. It is recorded that Manila and the Philippines had trade relations with most neighboring countries at least as far back as the ninth to twelfth centuries. The port was also the staging point for the Manila galleons, a state-monopolized shipping line running to Acapulco, Mexico and back, which operated virtually continuously from the sixteenth to early nineteenth centuries.

After the reclamation of mangrove swamp at the bayside of Manila, American construction firms developed the Port District across Malecon Drive (now Bonifacio Drive) from Intramuros. A new network of streets was laid out and piers were built.

Port District School 1910-1923

SDB outgrew the schoolhouse in Intramuros. In 1910, the government allocated to SDB a bungalow-type building of twenty-seven rooms upon

Front Gate of Port District School

a forty-acre tract along Malecon Drive between 12th and 16th Streets. The new school, once Spanish medical college, was located just a few blocks from its former Intramuros site — and one hundred yards from breezy Manila Bay. The building was large and low, with delightfully cool, long airy rooms, a large three-sided veranda with many hanging baskets and flowers everywhere, and a beautiful, well-kept lawn and gardens. The building was thoroughly furnished and in running order.

Classes for the Blind

After his return from California in 1910, Rogerio Lagman started teaching blind students at the school. None of them originally spoke English, yet they were cannily able to imitate Delight's voice perfectly even down the hall. Teachers from public schools once came to the school to investigate how the blind students spoke perfect English. The school educators disagreed on how to teach English to Filipinos: through native dialects or directly without them. The students were taught their dialects.

Charles Rice and Delight Rice
conversing with a mother and a prospective student

Students, circa 1918

When they reached school maturity, they were apprenticed as telephone operators and piano tuners. The others attended Manila High School, and one eventually became a minister and another a teacher. One of Delight's favorite statements was, "No student left the school without a job."

Braille Textbooks

Rogerio helped Delight produce Braille textbooks during school vacations. They both painstakingly transcribed textbooks into Braille with help from two Braille writers and then bound the books.

Vocational Training

In addition to academics, the deaf boys performed household duties as well as barbering, carpentry work, gardening and poultry-raising. They also built an irrigation system with a forty-horsepower stationary engine. The girls were taught sewing, dressmaking, hat-making and lace-making. They produced a high number of clothes, towels and curtains for the school's use and also did a large amount of mending.

Students at Port District School

The school gradually produced self-supporting bakers, cooks, printers, shoemakers, tailors and seamstresses. Two boys passed the regular civil service examination and were employed with the Bureau of Printing.

Reception for Government Officials

On January 5, 1912, distinguished members of the Commission and the Assembly were invited to a reception at SDB where children presented their class work and exercises. Guests included Governor General W. Cameron Forbes, Captain Holmes, Vice Governor N.W. Gilbert, Mr. and Mrs. Wilson, the former Governor L. Osorio of Cavite, Speaker Sergio Osmena, Director Frank R. White, Mrs. Victoriana Mapa, Mrs. Jaime de Veyrn, and about forty Assembly members. After the presentation, refreshments made by the pupils were served.

Boy Scouts Troop 2

Delight formed the BSA Troop 2 (later Troop 85), one of the earliest troops in the Philippines. The girls sewed all of their uniforms. One day the twenty boys of this troop gave a demonstration. Seven tenderfeet performed first aid and signaling. An older scout, Jose Firme, started a fire without using matches, even if it was lightly raining.

Athletic Meets

Delight established the first athletic meet in school history. The boys were divided into four teams: greens, blues, reds, and yellows. Each team was composed equally of both blind and deaf boys so they could help each other. The activities included the fifty- and hundred-yard dashes, the high jump and pastimes such as a rooster fight, Indian wrestling, and tug-of-war. The rivalry was entirely between the teams they represented, not the deaf students and the blind students. In the first meet a blind boy won the fifty- and hundred-yard dashes. A deaf boy won the high jump, with a blind boy in a close second.

To make it possible for the blind boys to run, wires were stretched along the course and handles attached. The boys then were able to guide themselves using their sense of touch, running as well as the deaf boys. One of the students' favorite games was Pick-a-Back. The players ran from one goal to another, carrying other players on their backs. The blind boys knew what to do and where to go by listening to the teachers' directions. The deaf boys were directed through hand signs. The school also defeated other schools in several competitions, especially in volleyball.

Screened Classroom Outside the Main Building

Port District School Dining Room

Growing Enrollment

In November 1919, Delight wrote to the *Silent Worker:*

> *I work just twenty hours a day. Teach two classes five hours, have twenty-five deaf children for oral work extra, run the house, supervise the native teachers and am putting six blind students through the Manila High School by reading their lessons at night.*

Delight's hard work paid off. In October 1920, SDB started its fourteenth year with fifty-one deaf pupils and twenty-six blind pupils. Twenty-one of the deaf students were under the age of seven. This was the largest enrollment in school history; the deaf and blind education was no longer an experiment. More and more parents were anxious to enroll their little children, but the school dormitories were so crowded that new applicants had to be turned away. That situation necessitated the government's authorization of funds for the construction of a new larger school in Pasay City.

Surprise Visit

In 1921, Governor-General Leonard Wood paid SDB a surprise visit. After his inspection tour, he said that the school was the cleanest in the public school system throughout the country.

Final Farewell

Due to ill health in 1922, a doctor advised Delight to return to California. On the evening of January 14, 1923, Delight was honored with a farewell party given by the Mother Delight Rice Literary Society, the Dr. Marqudet Literary Society, and BSA Troop 2. *The Manila Times* published:

> *A difficult work this, and not accomplished, one may be sure, without infinite self-sacrifice and patience; but a great work, for by it little deaf and blind children are led back to a world from which nature and man once exclude them.*

On January 16, 1923, SDB teachers, pupils and workers, filled with lamentation, accompanied Delight in a parade to a pier. She, along with pupils Bernardo Cuengco and Lester Naftaly, boarded a waiting USAT ship. The sorrowful staff remained at the wharf watching the departing ship until it disappeared from Manila Bay.

Delight Rice on the School Veranda

School Groups

The Life Story of Mother Delight Rice and Her Children

Class of 1918

Graduating Class

Vocational Training

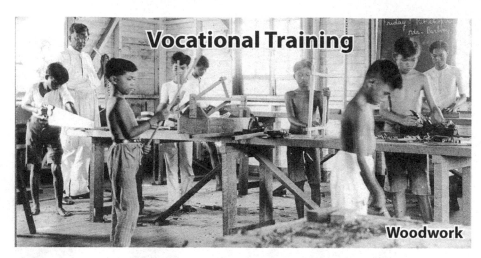

Woodwork

Sewing

Dyeing Work

The Life Story of Mother Delight Rice and Her Children

Horticulture

School's Self-Supporting Garden

Flower Cutting

Fresh Produce

Charles Rice Overseeing Gardeners

Sports

Practice Field on the Future Site of Rizal Park
The Manila Hotel in background

Boxing

Tug-of-War

Athletic Meet

Practice Field

The Life Story of Mother Delight Rice and Her Children

Boy Scouts

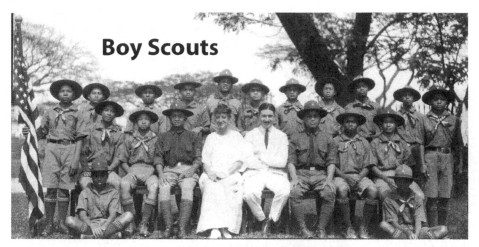

Boy Scouts of America Troop 2

School Driveway

Camping

Pasay School
on F.B. Harrison Street

Charles Rice at entrance
of the newly completed
school building in 1923

**Pasay School
1923-Present**

Charles Rice
at the entrance

Historical Fact: Pasay City

Pasay City was one of Metro Manila's original four cities. Due to its proximity to Manila, it quickly became an urban town during the American rule. It is now one of the sixteen cities that make up Greater Manila.

The name of Pasay may have originated from the Spanish *paso hay,* meaning *there is a pass.* This referred to the paths cleared among the grass leading to the southern parts from Manila.

Pasay School 1923-Present

In 1920, the government appropriated a 260,000-peso (US $130,000) fund for the construction of a large two-storied, semi-concrete building on a five-acre lot anonymously donated by an American woman.

In June 1923, SDB was relocated to its present location along F.B. Harrison Street in Pasay City. It once had access to Manila Bay for salt-water bathing and was also sufficiently close for cultivating a large garden for school use.

Last American Principals

After Delight's departure, SDB's last two American principals were Julia Hayes (1923-1936) and Lucretia Belting (1936-1940). The native officers-in-charge took over in 1940-1941.

Julia Hayes was born in Fulton, Kentucky, on October 13, 1875. Her death date and place remain unknown.

Lucretia Belting was born in the small town of Illiopolis near Springfield, Illinois, on September 19, 1881 to Prussian-born father Theo. She was a long-time teacher in Duluth, Minnesota, until she retired to Daytona, Florida. She died in Lafayette, Indiana, in March 1971.

Farewell Party for Lucretia Belting, Last American Principal
March 20, 1941

Principal Julia Hayes

Hired as a new principal by the Bureau of Education director, Julia Hayes lacked experience in deaf or blind education. On June 28, 1923, *The Manila Times* reported that teachers staged a walkout due to their clash with her. Charles Rice also found it impossible to work with her, so he resigned from the school after twelve years. He returned to California in October 1923 and joined Delight.

Japanese Occupation

During the Japanese occupation of 1941-1945, the school was closed and the Japanese troops were quartered there, causing considerable damage. Consequently, many invaluable documents were lost.

Pure Oral Method

After the war, SDB reopened with seventy-three students on November 18, 1946. Its first native principal was Maria Francisco (1946-60). Newly trained educators introduced the pure oral method. In 1973,

SAID executive director Carl A. Argila gave a reading test to select SDB graduates. He found them functionally illiterate because their reading levels were lower than grade two. This was blamed on the pure oral method. In other words, the needless overstressing of lipreading and speech hindered the basic learning process of reading, writing and arithmetic.

Separation of the School

In June 1963, Philippine law mandated that SDB be separated into two schools: the newly named Philippine School for the Deaf (PSD) and Philippine National School for the Blind (PNSB). PSD remains at its current compound. It is the only government-owned institution of its kind in the Philippines and also the only public day-residential school for the deaf.

Aftermath

Things sadly changed following Delight's departure. Her influence of American Sign Language (ASL) remains strong at the school, though. The emergence of oralism after the war eventually spawned new deaf private schools practicing ASL during the 1960s and 1970s.

Liza Martinez, Ph.D., the director of Philippine Deaf Resource Center, and Rafaelito Abat, a deaf researcher, are in the process of developing a national sign language, Filipino Sign Language (FSL). They have been urging the Department of Education to include FSL in curricula, despite controversial resistance from the deaf community. The resistance stems from the deeply rooted usage of ASL in the Philippines for over one hundred years. This is akin to how, in 1973, the government changed the country's official language from English to Filipino, the formal name of Tagalog. Yet, the natives continue to speak English even today.

California School
for the Deaf
in Berkeley

**California
School
for the Deaf**

**Bear Hunt Sculpture by Douglas Tilden
at California School for the Deaf in Fremont**

Chapter 5

CALIFORNIA SCHOOL FOR THE DEAF

Historical Fact

The first class at California School for the Deaf (CSD) began on May 1, 1860, with three pupils. The class, taught by H.B. Crandall, took place in a rented house at 15 Tehama Street in San Francisco. Crandall, himself deaf, came from New York School for the Deaf in White Plains. In 1861, CSD was relocated southward across the city to a newly completed schoolhouse on the corner of Mission and Sparks (now 16th) Streets. It was again moved in 1869, eastward across the San Francisco Bay to a larger building on a 130-acre campus at Warring and Parker Streets in Berkeley. Its final resting place, as of 1980, is the ninety-one-acre site on Gallaudet Drive and Stevenson Boulevard in Fremont.

Alumni Legends

Theophilus d'Estrella (1851-1929), Class of 1873
Acclaimed teacher, writer, artist, photographer, traveller, and mentor to Douglas Tilden and Granville Redmond

Douglas Tilden (1860-1935), Class of 1879
World-class sculptor of "The Michelangelo of the West" and co-founder of the California Association of the Deaf

Granville Redmond (1871-1935), Class of 1890
Prominent California landscape painter and master of colors, and scenery backstage screen painter and actor at Charlie Chaplin's movie studio

Robert Davila (1932-present), Class of 1948
President of Gallaudet University (2007-2009), Director of National Technical Institute for the Deaf (1996-2006), Vice President of Rochester Institute of Technology (1996-2006), and Assistant Secretary for Special Education and Rehabilitation Services of U.S. Department of Education (1989-1993)

Joel Barish (1968-present), Class of 1986
*Founder and CEO of DeafNation, host of DeafNation Expo
(2003-present), DeafNation World Expo (2010-present), and "No Barrier
with Joel Barish," the documentary show on Deaf people and communities in
more than seventy-five countries (2006-present)*

Sean Virnig (1973-present), Class of 1992
*Superintendent of CSD (2011-present), Director of Education at Texas
School for the Deaf (2010-2011), and founder-owner of Rawland Cycles,
customized bicycle fabricator*

SDB Teachers and Students Sent to CSD by Delight Rice

Rogerio R. Lagman

Rogerio Lagman passed the competitive examination and was sent to
CSDB in September 1909. An interesting and intelligent young blind
man, his objective for the year was to learn teaching methods for blind
pupils.

**Rogerio R.
Lagman**

Rogerio was Delight's first blind student and had great
influence at SDB. He persevered and, with Delight's
coaching, took the civil service examination especially
for American teachers. He achieved the highest grades
in that particular class. Delight expected him to get
paid as much as the American teachers, but the director
of Bureau of Education decided that such a salary was
not for Filipinos. Rogerio promptly resigned from
teaching, a big blow to Delight as well as her school.
He immediately turned to business, prospered rapidly and made income
easily surpassing the salary of the American teaching position. He
employed blind people as well as deaf people. He later was the president
of United Assembly of the Blind in the Philippines.

Francisca Lagman

Francisca Lagman was Rogerio Lagman's younger sister and faithful
companion. In 1910, Delight accompanied her to CSD to study deaf

education methods, and Francisca then taught the primary class at SDB. Delight could not have found a more willing, eager and bright assistant. Francisca married Jose Tesojo at the first wedding ceremony held in the SDB building on Malecon Drive and attended by all the pupils and twenty guests.

Francisca Lagman

Paula Felizardo

Paula Felizardo (later Gutierrez) was Delight's first pupil. Delight accompanied her to CSD in January 1914. After a brief marriage to a hearing native in San Francisco, Paula returned to Manila on May 5 that same year. Delight was hopeful Paula would enroll at Gallaudet College but was disappointed. Paula, using fingerspelling and classical signs without mouthing, offered no insight when interviewed by Peace Corps consultant Frances Parsons on why she did not attend Gallaudet.

Paula was the founding secretary of Philippine Association of the Deaf (PAD) in 1926-1935. On the morning of August 1, 1970, she was honored as the first SDB alumna to type the first international message to Robert Lankenau, the 1968-1972 president of National Association of the Deaf in the United States, at the historic inauguration of a new teletypewriter (TTY) network in the Philippines.

Paula Felizardo

Pedro C. Santos

Born in the capital of Malolos City in Bulacan Province in 1900, Pedro Santos enrolled at CSD in 1919 after graduating from SDB. He wrote the *Philippine Citizen* articles for the school's *California News* publication. He worked as a boys' dormitory monitor at Moss Hall. He then attended Kendall School in Washington, D.C., and graduated on June 13, 1922. Although popular knowledge had it that he attended Gallaudet College, official records show that Pedro was unable to attend the college because his three-year study-abroad contract with the Philippines Bureau of Education expired.

Pedro C. Santos

Pedro eventually returned to Manila to teach grades three and four at SDB and to supervise the BSA Troop 2 as its assistant scoutmaster. On October 17, 1923, he founded PAD. He served as its president in 1926-1935, 1938-1941, 1943-1945 and 1949-1950, executive director in 1951-1956, first vice president in 1965, and board member in 1966.

Bernardo Cuengco

On August 20, 1904, Bernardo "Sonny" Cuengco was born in the *barangay* (village) of Betis near the capital of San Fernando in Pampanga Province. He lost his hearing at the age of three, and enrolled at SDB two years later. As a little boy, he recited in signs more nursery rhymes than most American children ever knew. He became one of Delight's favorite pupils. He supervised boys' work at a poultry house for five years. For recreation he turned to boxing although Delight did not encourage his interest. During Governor-General Leonard Wood's visit at the school, he showed Bernardo short-hand jabs, and Delight finally did not object.

During the school break of 1922, Bernardo was the first deaf amateur boxer in Pampanga and knocked out three hearing boxers. As a result, he was called "Dempsey" after the renowned American boxer. He spent thirteen years at SDB and one year at Ateneo de Manila College (now University).

Bernardo Cuengco

In January 1923, Delight accompanied Bernardo and his schoolmate Lester Naftaly to California, where both attended CSD in Berkeley. Bernardo wrote articles for *The California News* and worked at a printing shop in the afternoons. He took the Gallaudet College entrance examination in May 1924, and graduated from CSD a year later. Delight had high hopes that he would attend the college and return to the Philippines as a role model. To her dismay, he was rejected because the college admitted only whites at that time.

After graduation, Bernardo worked in a printing office in San Francisco. Trained by Delight's brother Freeman, he was a professional lightweight boxer in 1925, but had to give up boxing due to old football injuries.

When Bernardo was in Manila for a visit, the U.S. Congress passed the bill to change the status of the Philippines from possession to commonwealth in order to grant them an ultimate independence. This forced him stay there for four more years, as he struggled to obtain a newly designated visa to return to the United States. He was the founding PAD vice president in 1926-1930. After a Philippine Silent Athletic Association banquet in honor of Gallaudet Day, Bernardo participated in a meeting that led to the making of a new all-deaf organization, *Mother Delight Society*, as a remembrance to their beloved friend, teacher and benefactor.

After returning from the Philippines, Bernardo worked as a linotypist at a printing shop in Berkeley. Since he always considered Delight as Mother Delight, he faithfully lived with her in the San Francisco Bay area for thirty-four years. Regardless of his birth under the American flag, he was not eligible for citizenship until World War II. He served as treasurer for East Bay Club for the Deaf (EBCD) in Oakland for ten years, and he was known for his meticulous work.

Delight did not approve of Bernardo's relationship with Nora, a deaf Caucasian woman, and eventually introduced him to Rose Fong at her parents' Chinatown tenement in San Francisco. Rose was a 1934 CSD graduate and 1939 Gallaudet graduate. After a short courtship, she and Bernardo married on May 3, 1947. The wedding reception was held at Delight's Blake Street residence. They had a son, Bernardo, Jr. and a daughter, Maria, both hearing. They happily resided in Berkeley for the rest of their lives.

Lester Naftaly

Lester Naftaly was born in Manila to Jewish Russian immigrants. In hopes of restoring his hearing, his mother hired a stunt pilot to fly him above Manila, with disappointing results. He then attended SDB.

In January 1923, Delight took Lester and Bernardo to San Francisco, where they enrolled at CSD. Lester graduated from CSD in June 1931, and attended Gallaudet College as a member of the Class of 1936 for three years. Back home in San Francisco, he worked with deaf employees at Blindcraft, also known as Lighthouse for the Blind, before joining two deaf workers in a tannery in Redwood City.

On December 19, 1937, Lester married his schoolmate, Jennie Ghera of Oakland, at the Little Chapel of the Flowers in Berkeley. None other than Delight interpreted their ceremony, and immediately following, a reception was held at her residence. The newlyweds lived in Redwood City.

Lester Naftaly

Lester's parents continued to reside in Manila for many years. In the spring of 1941, his mother underwent a brain tumor removal operation in the U.S., returning to the Philippines prior to the Japanese invasion. Both parents were imprisoned at the University of Santo Tomas internment camp in Manila. She died from pneumonia there in June 1944; he was freed a few months later.

For twenty-nine years, Lester worked as a radial drill press operator at United Centrifugal Pumps in San Jose until his retirement in 1977. He and Jennie lived in Alameda and then Oakland. Two years after Jennie's passing in 1990, he remarried to Norma Hensley. They lived in Walnut Creek and then moved to her hometown of Austin, Texas.

Author's Note: *Delight told the author that she asked a Catholic priest and a Jewish rabbi to instruct respective religions to her, and then she taught the religions to Bernardo and Lester respectively. During a family reunion in Ohio, she was once told that she would be blessed to heaven for teaching Catholicism to Bernardo, but that she would be damned to hell for teaching Judaism to Lester.*

Local Students Recommended to CSD by Delight Rice

George Attletweed

Born 1930 in Oakland, George Attletweed grew up in Berkeley. Delight spotted the eight-year-old in a public school while making her rounds. He was classified as mentally retarded because he did not speak. Delight determined that he was deaf, and recommended that his parents have him attend CSD. He breezed through the school and graduated in 1947. George attended Gallaudet College with the Class of 1952, but left to work as a printer in 1949. He eventually went back to school and received a bachelor's degree in 1966 and a master's degree in 1974 from San Francisco State University (SFSU). He worked on his doctorate at the University of California and SFSU. He taught deaf children in the San Jose Unified School District for six years, and worked as a professor and counselor at Ohlone College in Fremont. In 1972, he was appointed the first dean of the Deaf Studies program at Ohlone.

For many years, George was co-producer and editor of a weekly news service, *Dial-A-News (DAN)*. He also was board president for DEAF Media. Additionally, he co-hosted an Emmy Award-winning weekly television program, *The Silent Perspectives*, for five years.

George Attletweed

George was active with California Association of the Deaf (CAD). In 1962, he was one of the deaf community leaders who established the East Bay Referral Agency for the Deaf, the forerunner of Deaf Counseling, Advocacy & Referral Agency (DCARA), and was one of its first board members. He was the first secretary of CSD Alumni Association (CSDAA), the first deaf person appointed by Governor George Deukmejian to the Advisory Commission on Special Education (1983-1991), and was its chairperson (1987-88) and vice chairperson (1989-1990).

Ronald Hirano

Born in Berkeley, California, in 1932, Ronald Hirano was diagnosed as deaf when he was an infant. His parents were recommended by their doctor to see Delight for consultation. The first time she saw Ronald, he was in a cradle. That was the beginning of his lifetime relationship with her.

Delight recommended that Ronald be admitted to CSD nearby. He started attending there as a day pupil in 1938 and commuted from his family residence at 2809 California Street until April 1942 when his entire family was ordered to be evacuated to internment camps along with 120,000 Japanese-Americans from the Pacific Coast. His father asked Delight to take over Ronald's guardianship, and she agreed. With a special permit card issued by the FBI, Ronald continued commuting

Ronald Hirano

between her Berkeley home at 2149 Blake Street and the CSD. He was active in school organizations and interscholastic sports. In 1952 he became the seventh Eagle Scout of BSA Troop 11. After his 1952 graduation from CSD, he went on to Gallaudet College, participated in intercollegiate sports and graduated in 1955.

For thirty-seven years, Ronald was successively employed as a drafter, engineer and project manager by several firms designing, fabricating and installing aluminum architectural products such as windows, curtain walls, doors and panels for commercial buildings and skyscrapers. He also served as an instructor at Ohlone College for two years and as a drafting and design technology instructor at SouthWest Collegiate Institute for the Deaf (SWCID) in Big Spring, Texas, for two years. He finally retired in 1995.

Ronald was an alpine leader of summer and winter backpacking and mountaineering treks for deaf and hearing hikers in California's High Sierra for sixteen years. He also owned a side business in income tax services for nineteen years.

Jeanette Davis

Jeanette Davis Daviton

In 1934, Delight visited Jeanette Davis' parents in the nearby city of Richmond, California. After observing the two-year-old's eyes, she indicated that their daughter was intelligent. She gave them a CSD brochure and encouraged them to have Jeanette admitted there. The six-year-old enrolled in 1938 and was Ronald's classmate from the first through the twelfth grades. After graduation in 1952, she married her schoolmate David Daviton. They had four deaf children, all of whom attended CSD.

Daniel Lynch

The son of prominent parents in Vallejo, California, Daniel Lynch became deaf from measles and whooping cough at the age of two. When he attended kindergarten at a hearing Catholic school in 1937, he did not make progress because he could not hear the instructions.

During a search, Daniel's concerned mother Evelyn found Delight and asked her to tutor him, which she did at the Lynch residence for the remaining school year. She once brought five-year-old Ronald Hirano with her, and after the session both boys played on when she discussed Daniel's education with Evelyn. She successfully convinced the mother to enroll him at CSD despite her strong support for speech and speechreading. His parents eventually became leaders in CSD's Association of Parents, Teachers and Counselors (APTC). Daniel was president of three school organizations during high school, and was selected as an All-American halfback among deaf school football teams around the nation. He graduated in 1953.

When Daniel enrolled at Gallaudet College, his mother phoned President Leonard Elstad to ask him to check on Daniel's continuing lipreading and speech training. Daniel graduated with an associate's degree and later bachelor's degree. He then earned a master's degree from SFSU. He spent thirty-four years teaching, coaching and mentoring deaf students at Colorado and California Schools for the Deaf. He played basketball for East Bay Club for the Deaf (EBCD).

Daniel Lynch

After his retirement, Daniel has continued being active in the deaf community. He successively served on the board of Bay Area Coalition of Deaf Senior Citizens (BACDSC) as vice president and president. He appointed Ronald Hirano editor of the BACDSC newsletter, *Senior Quest*, and was eventually succeeded by Ronald for the presidency. Theirs has been a lifelong friendship, as amazingly initiated by Delight.

Alice Rice Carrying
Paugliener Diki Diki

Moro dwarf
36 inches (91 cm) tall
at 41 years of age

Rice Family
1910-1923

Chapter **6**

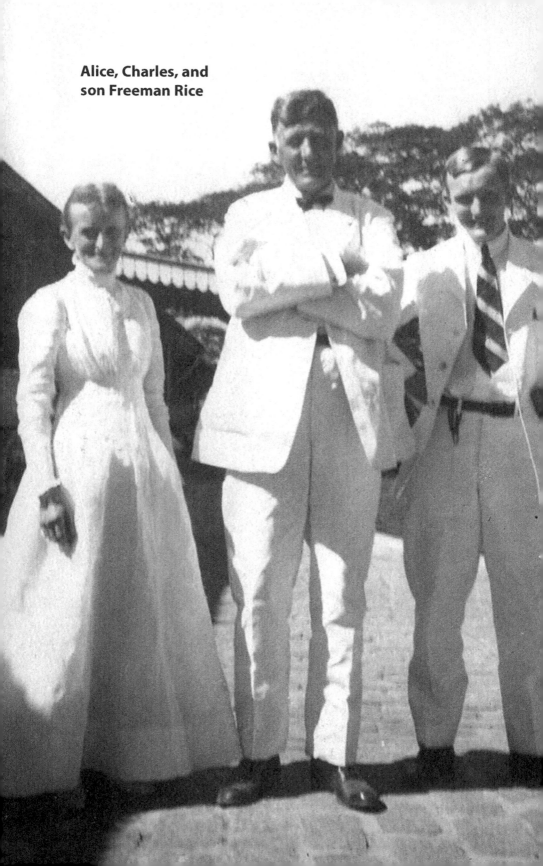

Alice, Charles, and son Freeman Rice

Chapter 6

RICE FAMILY 1910-1923

1910 Vacation

In 1910, Delight returned to the United States for a three-month vacation. Accompanied by her father Charles, she gave a lecture about the Philippines and her school in Columbus on May 13, then in Chicago on May 20, and then in Delavan, Wisconsin, on May 21. The lecture at Columbus was under the auspices of the Columbus division of National Fraternal Society of the Deaf (NFSD), of which Charles was a member. The lecture at Chicago was sponsored by the NFSD Chicago division, and the one in Delavan was addressed to pupils at the WSD chapel. Later that evening, she gave another speech at a church.

Charles soon gave up his position as a clerk at the Ohio State Insurance Board in Columbus to accompany Delight back to Manila. Her mother Alice and brothers Percy and Freeman moved to Manila in November 1910. Charles was employed as a clerk at the Bureau of Education in Manila from 1910 to 1914.

Marriage

On February 7, 1911, Delight Rice and Ralph G. Webber were married in Hong Kong. Ralph, a graduate of Bowdoin College in Brunswick, Maine, went to the Philippines to engage in the banking business five years earlier. Unfortunately, their marriage did not last long. On November 27, 1915, he sued her for divorce in the State of Maine Superior Court because he claimed her utter desertion continued for three years. That was due to her very strong devotion to the deaf and blind children at SDB.

Author's Note: *Delight Rice once told the author that Ralph called her beloved pupils "deef," meant to offend.*

Love Affairs

In 1958, PAD president and SDB alumnus Richard West visited Delight in California. He later told the author about her secret love affairs with American government officials and military officers. When the author lived at her Berkeley residence, she displayed numerous Oriental metal items such as Buddha-type bronze statuettes and a large brass Samovar (Russian teapot). He initially believed she bought them on her Asian travels until Richard said otherwise: that her secret lovers gifted them to her.

Infante Jaime, Duke of Segovia

Delight was considered for the position of instructor to Infante Jaime, Duke of Segovia (1908-1975), the second deaf son of King Alfonso XIII of Spain (1886-1941). Although she was not ultimately selected, her application was newsworthy for the Manila newspapers.

Diki Diki

Alice Rice met the renowned forty-one-year-old "Moro dwarf," Paugliener Diki Diki, who measured thirty-six inches tall. She conversed with him through five interpreters, each using a different dialect. She coaxed him to be photographed until he finally budged to be held like a baby during the photo session.

1914 Vacation

In 1914, Delight left the Philippines for the United States to recover from exhaustion. During her brief absence, Charles took over as interim principal of SDB. After she placed Paula Felizardo at CSD, Delight rested up in Southern California. She attended local parties and socialized with deaf women there.

On June 25-July 2, 1914, she attended the Twentieth Convention of American Instructors for the Deaf (CAID) at Virginia School for the Deaf in Staunton. She presented, in signs, about her school work in the Philippines. In a photo session, she sat next to Dr. Percival Hall, the second president of Gallaudet College (1910-1945), with a group of school superintendents and principals.

**Delight Rice and Dr. Percival Hall (on her right)
at the 20th CAID on June 25-July 2, 1914**
Virginia School for the Deaf in Staunton

Relocation to California

In 1914, the new Governor-General Francis B. Harrison made many changes in the Philippines, including replacing the American officers and teachers with educated natives. Consequently, Charles was transferred from his clerk position to his wife Alice's teaching and supervising position at SDB. She lost the job and moved to Berkeley, California, with their son Freeman.

In December 1914, Alice stayed in Millbrae as a guest of Mr. and Mrs. W. E. Gore. After shopping in San Francisco, she carried a heavy bag of silverware as she stepped aboard a streetcar. She missed her footing and signaled two well-dressed men to help her up. One of them stole her bag, but a keen conductor quickly took it from the thief and returned it

Alice Rice and her sons Freeman and Percy

to Alice. When the streetcar approached Daly City, police cars overtook and surrounded the streetcar. The police arrested, handcuffed and hauled the two men into a police wagon. The conductor told the scared Alice that they committed larceny or pick-pocketing. She then rode safely to Millbrae.

One cold evening in January 1915, Alice Rice warmed herself near a gas heater at her residence at 2127 Ashby Avenue in Berkeley. Her dress caught afire and in an instant, her whole back was aflame. She shrieked and rushed toward where her son Freeman slept. He quickly threw three blankets upon his mother and successfully smothered the flames. Alice gradually recovered from her serious burns.

On April 14, 1915, Alice invited twenty people for a luncheon at her Ashby Street home. Its purpose was a fundraising raffle for the eleventh NAD convention in San Francisco during the 1914-1915 Pacific-Panama International Exposition.

On August 19, 1917, Alice invited deaf people to a social in honor of her guest Anna Johnson, one of Delight's deaf-blind pupils at WSD. During the social, Samuel Bean talked with Anna for hours. He said she was a dandy talker with an impeccable flow in her language.

1916 Presidential Election

The 1916 U.S. presidential election was a contest between the incumbent president, Woodrow Wilson (D) and U.S. Supreme Court Justice Charles Hughes (R). The result was exceptionally close and the outcome was in doubt for several days.

Delight always remained an ardent Republican supporter. In the Philippines, the newspapers announced Hughes a winner. That evening, she partied with American government officials and military officers at a Republican victory celebration in Manila. The next morning, the newspapers announced Wilson a winner instead and everyone was stunned.

Suiting the Occasion

Delight wrote that she was surprised to find a portrait of Dr. Thomas Hopkins Gallaudet in the assembly room of a school for deaf students when she and her father visited Tokyo in 1919. *The Silent Worker* stated:

The Japanese make many beautiful ceremonies of the little things of life. For instance, in serving tea they have what is known as the "Ceremonial Tea." This ceremony carries many delightful customs. For example, but one picture, which is quite simple, is hung in the room and is selected as to create beautiful thoughts in the mind of the guest. While looking at the picture the guest is supposed to concentrate, mediate and get from it the beautiful thoughts the host desires as he has taken great pains to consider all the individual characteristics of the guest and has tried to select something which will fill him with good desires. This principle is applied in decorating the home and the school.

When Miss Delight Rice and her father visited the School for the Deaf at Tokyo, they were much surprised to see hanging on the wall a picture of Thomas Hopkins Gallaudet. Later, when Mr. John D. Wright visited the same school, he found hanging on the wall a picture of Dr. Alexander Graham Bell. Not being acquainted with the Japanese customs, friends of Mr. Wright thought that Miss Rice was too prejudiced to see the other picture and friends of Miss Rice thought that Mr. Wright was so narrow that he would not mention seeing the picture of Gallaudet. The fact is neither saw the other picture. The Japanese in advance considered the tastes of their guests and concluded that the picture of Dr. Bell would create pleasure in the mind of Mr. Wright and that the picture of Dr. Gallaudet would create beautiful thoughts in the minds of Miss Rice and her father and accordingly the particular picture was placed on the wall for the benefit of the guest.

This incident illustrates the point that many of the delightful customs of the Japanese are easily misunderstood.

Author's Note: *Gallaudet supported sign language while Bell opposed it in favor of oralism. This controversy persists to the present day.*

American Intervention in Siberia

In 1919, Delight resigned from her position as SDB principal. She went to Vladivostok in far eastern Russia as a Red Cross nurse for the American Expeditionary Force Siberia during the Russian Civil War. She was engaged to marry an U.S. Army officer in Siberia, although records do not show them having proceeded with the marriage. Meanwhile, her father took over the principal's position, and her mother Alice came back from California to help him out. Delight later returned to Manila and resumed her work at SDB.

Author's note: *The first U.S. Army troops, including 2,800 officers and enlisted men from the 27th and 31st Infantry Regiments stationed in the Philippines, were sent to Siberia from August 15, 1918 to April 1, 1920.*

Alice Rice's Passing

Alice died at age of sixty-one from apoplexy in Manila on October 3, 1920 after several months of illness. She lived in Manila for about three years and was the matron of SDB. She was sweet-tempered and always very good to the children.

Alice Rice

Audiological testing
in Los Angeles
during the 1950s

Chapter **7**

Rice Family
1923-1964

Audiological testing in Berkeley during the 1930s

Chapter 7

RICE FAMILY 1923-1964

Voyage to San Francisco

During very stormy weather, Delight narrowly escaped death on the rocking voyage of USAT *Thomas*. Since the departure from Manila on January 16, 1923, she was dazed by the almost continuous storms. One night as she stepped out of the recreation hall, a lurch of the ship sent her hurtling across the deck. She fell and her head was caught between the boat rail and the deck so tightly that members of the ship's crew had to remove the railing with axes to release her. As the *Thomas* approached Chinwangtao (now Qinhuangdao), China, its rudder was damaged by ice at the entrance. The ship finally arrived in San Francisco on February 15.

Bernardo Cuengco, Delight Rice and Lester Naftaly

San Mateo County

Upon arrival, Delight was taken straight home and bedridden for several months. She had a nervous shock and hemorrhaging in her ear that caused a permanent loss of her sense of smell.

Author's note: *In the early 1960s, I visited her at her Berkeley residence. Upon entry, I smelled gas vapor; she had forgotten to turn off the gas on her stove. I immediately turned it off and opened the windows.*

Bernardo, Charles Rice and Lester
Palo Alto, California, 1923

After moving from an icebox-like house in Menlo Park in 1923, Delight lived with Bernardo and Lester in a new, cozy house at 167 Webster Street in Palo Alto. It contained a large backyard garden with fruit trees. She cooked and canned the fruits. She was employed in the food research department at nearby Stanford University. In October, her father Charles moved from Manila to join them. In March 1924, they again relocated from Palo Alto to a ten-room house in Burlingame.

San Francisco

For a few years, Delight resided with her father in San Francisco. In 1924, she received a special certificate for teaching lipreading classes at the now-defunct Gough School for the Oral Deaf in San Francisco.

Berkeley Public Schools

On September 18, 1928, the Berkeley Public Schools (now Unified School District) Board of Education voted to inaugurate special classes for hard of hearing children and to appoint Delight teach them at an annual salary of $2,460 upon Superintendent Lewis Smith's recommendation. She began teaching the children within two weeks of relocating from San Francisco.

In October 1928, Delight surveyed hard of hearing children in the Berkeley public schools. Her study indicated that slight hearing defects and speech impediments produced timidity that could affect their entire lives. On March 8, 1929, Delight tested more than one hundred hard of hearing children from three Berkeley public schools using an audiometer that measured their hearing levels. The audiometer, on loan from the San Francisco Board of Education, was the only one of its kind in the Bay Area and probably one of four in California at that time.

In the spring of 1930, Delight was in charge of lipreading instruction at twelve schools with thirty-nine pupils. The classes were held twice a week with lipreading lessons averaging twenty to thirty minutes each. Within three years, other public schools referred two hundred hard of hearing children to her for instruction. Her instruction was in such great demand, as evidenced by a long waiting list.

During the school year of 1931-1932, Delight provided audiological testing to 2,150 children from kindergarten through grade three for the first time in school history. She also devised a method of testing young children to supplement written tests given to older pupils and thus paved the way for its introduction to other schools. That new method replaced the previously tedious ones. Dr. Harvey Fletcher (1884-1981), acoustical research director for the Bell Telephone Laboratories and inventor of the audiometer and a hearing aid, officially commended her newly accomplished method.

The 1933 survey Delight conducted revealed one percent of the students were hard of hearing in comparison with the 1928 survey showing five percent.

Delight wrote:

The public is not aware of the fact that ear trouble starts in the young child. Detecting defective hearing is very difficult. The earlier this hearing defect is found and treated, or otherwise dealt with, the better for the child. 80 percent of these cases can be saved.

The aim of the department of lip reading is to detect deafness and prevent it if possible, to supplement education with lip reading so the child can get all the schools offer if the hearing impairment cannot be remedied, and to prepare the boys and girls for the future when they must go out and meet the difficulties of finding the right kind of work.

Many of our school children are hard of hearing. They are meeting these manifold difficulties now. They think in unhappy bewilderment as we, to our great discredit, have led them to think that they are woefully slow, or downright stupid, or no good somehow, and they plod along, aloof and hurt, misunderstanding and misunderstood. Often they defy the existing order into which they fit so poorly and become disciplinary cases, delinquents even; or still again, and this last is not at all among these lamentable occurrences, they work successfully on the whole and yet miss the excellences they might achieve, unaware of the fact of this failure or of the reason for it.

Delight was a supervisor in conservation of sight, hearing and speech in the Berkeley Public Schools system. She retired at the mandatory retirement age of sixty-five in 1949.

Charles Merrick Rice

Delight's father Charles was well known in the local deaf community as a respectable gentleman and for his kind deeds as well. His ready wits and interesting conversations made him a welcome guest wherever he went.

In the summer of 1929, Charles was injured in a streetcar accident and recuperated with friends by playing Whist, a card game. He was a host of a San Francisco bridge card club.

Charles passed away at the age of seventy-nine on October 16, 1933, after several months of failing health. Two days later, a funeral service in Berkeley was conducted by the Reverend George W. Gaertner. Delight gave, in sign language, a most beautiful rendition of "Crossing the Bar" and "Nearer My God to Thee," two of her father's favorite hymns. That marked the sad ending of her lifelong companionship with her father.

East Bay Club for the Deaf

In the December 12, 1941, issue of *The California News*, Wildey Meyers wrote:

Charles and Delight Rice

> *The deaf at large, and especially the local deaf people, have long had a valued friend in the person of Miss Delight Rice of Berkeley. As many of the recent improvements and benefits enjoyed by the East Bay Club (for the Deaf) have been largely due to her untiring efforts, the members decided to sponsor a little demonstration of their gratitude on Saturday evening, November 23. Miss Rice was innocently called to the platform to make some remarks, after which she was presented with an electric iron and an automatic electric toaster. She was taken very much by surprise and was deeply touched.*

In December 1943, Delight and Mrs. Edwin Driggs received a great deal of credit for interpreting the negotiations of the purchase of a two-story clubhouse on the corner of 22nd Street (now Grand Avenue) and Grove Street (now Martin Luther King, Jr. Way).

As co-sponsors and advisors, Delight and Mrs. Driggs assisted the reclamation and renovation of the clubhouse, which was decrepit and decaying due to neglect during the war years. Proceeds from shows and parties paid off the mortgage. A mortgage-burning ceremony was held at the newly remodeled clubhouse on May 25, 1946.

Tanforan Assembly Center

During the early days of World War II in the spring of 1942, the Tanforan Racetrack in San Bruno was hastily converted to the Tanforan Assembly Center to temporarily detain four thousand *Nikkei* (Japanese emigrants or descendants). They, along with 120,000 evacuees, were then transferred to ten hastily, sloppily constructed internment camps in the desolate western states during the late summer.

In May 1942, Delight drove nine-year-old Ronald Hirano to visit his family at Tanforan. They were shocked to find his family living in horse stables. His parents introduced a deaf internee who was a 1938 CSD graduate, Tadashi "Tad" Yamamoto.

Tad shared a terrifying story: When he lived in an apartment in Oakland, he was not aware of the evacuation order for Japanese-Americans that had been posted publicly in February 1942. One night FBI agents abruptly barged into his apartment, hauled him out quickly without allowing him time to pack, and drove him to Tanforan. It was at Tanforan that he met Ronald's parents, and he expressed gratitude for their donation of clothes and other essentials to him.

After the war, Tad repeatedly told Ronald of his appreciation for his parents' generosity. He spent his final days at a convalescent home in 1976-1980.

Tule Lake Internment Camp

The Tule Lake Internment Camp, located in the desolate northeast part of California, was specifically used to imprison Nikkei disloyal objectors after they refused to sign mandatory loyalty pledges.

In that spring, Delight urged eleven deaf Nikkei to go to the Tule Lake Internment Camp. The probable reason was its proximity to the San Francisco Bay Area or perhaps that it was Helen Keller School, the only internment camp including a school for the multi-handicapped. On May 12, 1943, 1940 CSD graduate Ruth Takagi was specifically transferred from the Manzanar Internment Camp in Southeastern California to assist Special Students Advisor Natalie Perry in organizing the program.

In the spring of 1943, Delight tried to convince Harvey M. Coverly, project director of Tule Lake Camp War Relocation Authority (WRA), to return deaf Nikkei children to CSD, to no avail. She then recommended a teacher to the Education Department of WRA, but she did not know what happened to that appointment. She unsuccessfully tried to volunteer helping deaf young internees at Tule Lake Camp during summer vacation.

Hirano Family at Topaz Internment Camp in Utah
Front row: Janet, Mother Mary, Baby Carol and Robert
Back row: Ronald, Delight Rice and Daniel. *Inset:* Father James

Topaz Internment Camp

The Topaz Internment Camp was located sixteen miles northwest of the small city of Delta in the west central desert area of Utah. It consisted of forty city blocks and its peak population was nine thousand, making it at one time the fifth largest city in Utah.

In the summer of 1944, Delight took eleven-year-old Ronald Hirano by train to visit his family at the internment camp. She went to nearby Delta for shopping, took some stamps from her war ration book to purchase rationed foods, and generously gave them to his family.

Ronald's father helped a deaf internee, Kazuko "Kay" Momii, enroll at Utah School for the Deaf in Ogden. After the war, she returned to CSD and graduated in 1951.

California Association of the Deaf

In August–September 1946, the fourteenth biennial CAD convention was held in Los Angeles. Delight spoke regarding the need for preschool nurseries for deaf children and requested assistance from the CAD. Apparently, no action was taken.

During the sixteenth biennial CAD Convention in Santa Monica, a sign language competition was held and Delight won fifth place for her inspiring rendition of Abraham Lincoln's Gettysburg Address.

Hearing Center of Metropolitan Los Angeles

Following her retirement from the Berkeley Public Schools, Delight was asked by Hearing Center of Metropolitan Los Angeles (HCMLA), an agency of the Community Chest, to demonstrate how to test the hearing of preschool children for six months. She eventually stayed on as a consultant for another ten years.

During those years, she tested the hearing of sixty thousand preschool children and supervised the follow-up program. She said, "The important part of this program is to learn of hearing defects before the child gets too old." A physician gave the children a more thorough examination at neighborhood clinics. Every six months Delight checked back on the children to learn whether the parents took the physician's advice or not. She finally retired again in 1959 at the age of seventy-five.

College of the Pacific

Even though she did not possess a college degree, Delight was selected over applicants with doctorate degrees for a summer position instructing an audiology course at College (now University) of the Pacific in Stockton. The reason was that she attended a normal school where they did not issue degrees other than teacher's certificates. She spent several summers there during her HCMLA employment breaks.

California Home for the Aged Deaf

Besides her job with the HCMLA, Delight was a resident manager of the three-storied house at 953 Menlo Avenue in Los Angeles. That residence, the California Home for the Aged Deaf (CHAD), accommodated six deaf elderly residents. It was once owned by the CAD. In 1965, it was eventually relocated eighteen miles east to its present site at 529 Las Tunas Drive in Arcadia.

Honorary Doctorate Degree of Pedagogy at Gallaudet College

On October 10, 1954, Agatha Tiegel Hanson of Oakland, California, wrote a letter asking Gallaudet College President Leonard Elstad to consider an honorary degree for Delight. She wrote:

Delight Rice and Ronald Hirano
receiving degrees
at Gallaudet College, 1955

This typewritten account is by no means all of Miss Rice's record. Ever since I have come to California, I have heard on all sides her praises. She is wholly unselfish, and has spent a lifetime in helping the deaf. She is always at their service. She is an accomplished sign maker, and is always in demand at conventions and other gatherings as an interpreter, and in many other ways her time, service, and money have been freely given.

On June 4, 1955, Delight was awarded an honorary doctorate degree in pedagogy during the ninety-first commencement at Gallaudet College. Coincidentally, Ronald Hirano graduated in the same ceremony. Dr. Elstad handed Ronald's degree to Delight, and she in turn handed it to him — an unprecedented move in Gallaudet history.

Philippine Visit

The Manila Times

SHE'S HOME—Dr. Delight Rice, founder of the School for the Deaf and Blind, gets a tearful welcome on her arrival yesterday after a 3½-year absence from the country. Dr. Rice is shown being greeted by some deaf and blind students, as well as faculty members of the school. She will return to her home in California after her visit here. (Story on page 2½-A)

News Photo of Delight Rice
at Manila International Airport

September 7, 1961 is the most awaited time of all deaf members, because it is the date that our most beloved and endeared Dr. Delight Rice is coming to visit the Philippines. Dr. Rice is the founder, pioneer, and the first teacher of the School for the Deaf and the Blind in the Philippines.
– The Silent Worker

Upon Delight's arrival at the Manila International Airport, three hundred students and alumni waved hands and placards reading *Welcome Most Beloved Mother Delight Rice.* It was a very sentimental scene when Delight, with open arms and tears in her eyes, met the surging crowd that hugged and greeted her. It was her first return to her beloved Philippines in thirty-eight years. Her visit was highlighted on the front pages of Manila's major newspapers.

Students and Alumni Greeting Delight Rice
at Manila International Airport, September 7, 1961

Delight was invited to stay at each of her former students' houses for a few days over several months. She was showered with awards and honors at many banquets hosted by SDB, the deaf and blind organizations, and the governmental agencies.

Delight planned to return home in December, but she could not resist the kind offer to extend her stay to March 1962 so that she could tour the country. On December 22, 1961, she was honored with the unveiling of a historical marker at SDB, as provided by the Historical Commission of the Philippine Government.

Richard S. West wrote:

The School for the Deaf and the Blind in Pasay which Dr. Rice founded fifty years ago will be the recipient of a historical marker from the Historical Commission of the Philippine Government honoring her as its only founder. Whatever else there was behind the picture, obviously the Philippine Government dug into its archives and found records to establish facts to credit Dr. Rice with pioneering the school.

On March 4, 1962, she was honored at a farewell banquet by the School for the Deaf Alumni Association. The next day, she departed Manila for a six-week tour visiting the deaf and blind schools in Asia and Europe. This trip was provided by the Philippine Board of Travel and Tourist Industry Commissioner of Tourism.

SDB graduate and PAD President Richard West, who visited Delight in California in 1958 and persuaded her to visit the Philippines, was instrumental in that hugely successful visit.

Delight Rice at the Literary Musical Program
School for the Deaf and the Blind, September 11, 1961

The Life Story of Mother Delight Rice and Her Children

Editha Bernardo and Friends, October 14, 1961

Florentino Pacheco and Family, October 16, 1961

Vincente Lopez and Friends, October 22, 1961

**Richard West
and Family**

**Maximiano de Guzman
and Friends**

Delight Rice Speaking
at the Luzon Association of the Deaf meeting

Farewell Banquet for Delight Rice
by the School for the Deaf Alumni Association, March 4, 1962

Unveiling of SDB Historical Marker, December 22, 1961
Maximiano de Guzman, Pres. of School for the Deaf Alumni Ass'n; Delight Rice;
Richard West, First Vice President; and Isauro Soriano, Secretary-Treasurer

Significant Generosity

Delight was renowned for her many kind contributions to the deaf community in California. She once donated a used 35mm movie projector to San Francisco Club for the Deaf for its regular use to show captioned films on loan. Whenever deaf people in need came to ask for her help, she never turned them down and often voluntarily interpreted for them.

On November 4, 1962, Ronald took Delight to EBCD for an address by WFD President Dragoljub "Drago" Vukotić of Yugoslavia (now Serbia). After his motivating speech, she wrote a $50 check and handed it to Vukotić to cover the organizational membership fee for her baby, Philippine Association of the Deaf. Everybody was stunned by her generosity.

Final Years in Berkeley

During the remaining years of her life, Delight quietly lived on the upper floor of Bernardo and Rose Cuengco's two-story residence at 2614B Grove Street (now Martin Luther King, Jr. Way) in Berkeley. Ronald faithfully visited her.

Delight passed away at the age of eighty-one at Shattuck-Carlton Convalescent Hospital in Berkeley at 5:40 a.m. on October 9, 1964. She was survived by her nephews, Charles "Bud" Rice and Robert E. Rice. Her funeral service at Berkeley Hills Chapel on October 11, 1964, was officiated by the Rev. Jack Finnegan of University Christian Church, where Delight regularly attended. Her remains were buried in the Rice Family plot at the Five Corners Cemetery in Milfordton Township, Ohio.

Death cannot efface the good she has done for us nor time dim the memory of a wonderful and influential personality.

– The California News

Inscription on the back side of the Rice Family Headstone

The Life Story of Mother Delight Rice and Her Children

Delight Rice
July 3, 1883-October 9, 1964

Front Entrance of Philippine School for the Deaf

Chapter

8

SCHOOL FOR THE DEAF AND THE BLIND
(1907)

PIONEER SCHOOL FOR THE
HANDICAPPED IN THE PHILIPPINES.
PLANNED BY DR. DAVID P. BARROWS,
DIRECTOR OF EDUCATION; ORGANIZED
BY MISS DELIA DELIGHT RICE, PRIN-
CIPAL TEACHER (1907-1923).
IT WAS ESTABLISHED IN THE CITY
OF MANILA WHERE IT REMAINED
UNTIL IT WAS TRANSFERRED TO
ITS PRESENT SITE IN PASAY CITY,
JUNE 1923.

LEADING INSTITUTION FOR THE
EDUCATION OF THE DEAF AND
THE BLIND IN THE PHILIPPINES.

Centennial
Celebration
2007

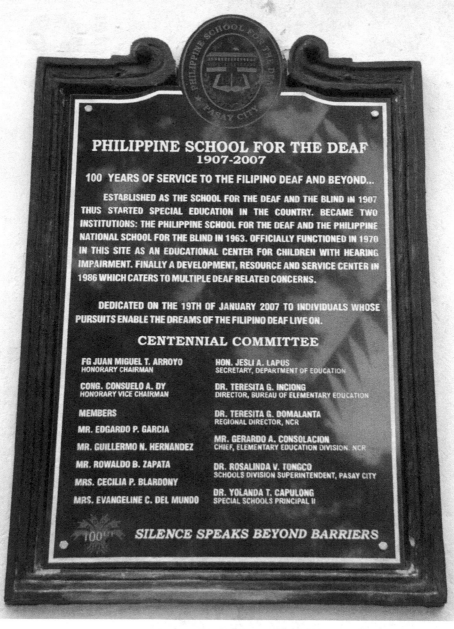

Centennial Historical Marker
at the Philippine School for the Deaf in Pasay City

The Life Story of Mother Delight Rice and Her Children

Chapter 8

CENTENNIAL CELEBRATION 2007

Launching of the Centennial Celebration

On January 19, 2007, the year-long Centennial Celebration at PSD in Pasay City was launched with an opening ceremony unveiling a centennial historical marker. The marker states:

100 Years of Service to the Filipino Deaf and Beyond...

Established as the School for the Deaf and Blind in 1907 thus started Special Education in the country. Became two institutions: the Philippine School for the Deaf and the Philippine National School for the Blind in 1963. Officially functioned in 1970 in this site as an educational center for children with hearing impairment. Finally, a development, resource and service center in 1986 which caters to multiple deaf-related concerns.

Dedicated on the 19th of January 2007 to individuals whose pursuits enable the dreams of the Filipino Deaf live on.

Susana Vergara Cofer

Unveiling of Centennial Historical Marker

Dignitaries and officials were present at the ceremony. The festivity was also highlighted with a presentation of the PSD hymn and a commemorative postage stamp.

Dignitaries and Officials

First Day Cover of SDB-PSD Centennial Postage Stamp

Conclusion of the Centennial Celebration

The celebration took place at PSD on December 1-9, 2007.

On December 5, PSD alumni Emmanuel and Maricris Galang emceed an outdoor ceremony on campus, attended by nine hundred local alumni and fifty overseas alumni and friends. Ronald Hirano gave a moving tribute to his foster mother, Delight Rice. On behalf of CSD Superintendent Henry Klopping, retired CSD teacher Stanley Smith presented a copy of the CSD history book to PSD principal Yolanda Capulong.

Workshops on various topics were presented at the Copacabana Hotel a few blocks from PSD. On December 8, CSD alumnus Chuck Hom and PSD/SAID alumna Anita Ortiz Ner coordinated a formal banquet at Heritage Hotel near PSD.

Maricris and Emmanuel Galang, Masters of Ceremony

Ronald Hirano and Emmanuel Galang
giving a tribute to Delight Rice

Stanley Smith, Principal Yolanda Capulong and Her Interpreter
presenting Dr. Henry Klopping's letter and CSD history book

The Life Story of Mother Delight Rice and Her Children

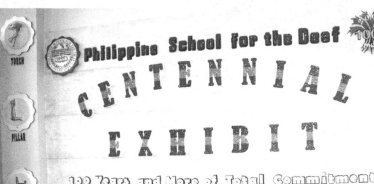

A Silent Worker on Focus
Ms. Delia Delight Rice
PSD Founder

SCHOOL FOR THE [D...]

Delight Rice

Delight Rice Visiting SDB, October 13, 1961

A F AND THE BLIND

Delight Rice's Timeline

**Delight Rice Accepting
the Plaque of Appreciation**
from the Parent-Teacher Association
of School for the Deaf and the Blind
on September 17, 1961

Delight Rice's Timeline

1880: On July 15, Delight's parents, Charles Rice and Alice Gregg, are married by Ohio School for the Deaf (OSD) Supt. Gilbert Otis Fay in Delaware, Ohio.

1883: On July 3, Delight is born on a farm in Milfordton Township, Ohio.

1886: Her family moves to Columbus, Ohio.

1901: She graduates from Central High School.

She applies for admission into Gallaudet College's Normal School, but is not accepted.

She interprets at the eleventh reunion of OSD Alumni Association in Columbus.

In September, she enters the Columbus Normal School (CNS).

She is trained on oral work by a speech supervisor at OSD in Columbus.

1903: On January 22, she graduates from CNS. In September, she starts teaching a special deaf-blind class at Wisconsin School for the Deaf (WSD) in Delavan.

1904: On December 27-30, she demonstrates a deaf-blind girl's successes at the fifty-second annual convention of the Wisconsin Teachers' Association in Milwaukee.

1905: In July, she presents *The Importance of Teaching the Blind-Deaf to Work* at the CAID, held at North Carolina School for the Deaf in Morganton.

1906: In May, she resigns from teaching at WSD and starts teaching two deaf-blind students at OSD in September.

1907: On January 23, she takes the civil service examination for teaching in the Philippines, and is the only successful applicant.

On May 3, she sails on the U.S. Army Transport *Thomas* from San Francisco for the Philippines and arrives in Manila on June 9.

She searches for two thousand deaf children around Manila and in the mountains.

She conducts an experimental work teaching four deaf pupils at Philippine Normal School.

She founds the Philippines' first deaf school (School for the Deaf and the Blind or SDB) on Calle Mercado in Ermita, Manila.

1908: She turns down an offer from the Chinese government to teach there.

She finds a SDB pupil is missing as a result of human sacrifice.

SDB moves to a second location on Calle Real del Palacio (now General Luna Street) in Intramuros, Manila.

1909: In September, SDB's first blind teacher Rogerio Lagman enrolls at California School for the Deaf and Blind (CSDB) in Berkeley.

1910: SDB again moves to a third location on Malecon Street (now Bonifacio Drive) between 12th and 16th Streets in Port District, Manila.

Delight admits Francisca Lagman, SDB's first hearing teacher.

On May 13, 20 and 21, she gives three well-publicized speeches in Columbus, Chicago and Delavan.

She accompanies her father Charles to Manila after his resignation from a clerical job in Columbus; her mother Alice and brothers move to Manila in November.

1911: On February 7, she marries banker Ralph Webber in Hong Kong.

1913: She is one of the applicants for teaching the second deaf son of Spain's King Alfonso XII. The son is Infante Jaime, Duke of Segovia.

1914: In May, she enrolls her first SDB pupil, Paula Felizardo, at California School for the Deaf (CSD).

On June 30-July 2, she gives a speech at the twentieth CAID at Virginia School for the Deaf in Staunton.

In December, her mother Alice moves to the San Francisco Bay Area after being laid off from her job at SDB.

1915: On November 15, Delight is sued by Ralph Webber for divorce in the Superior Court in Maine.

1919: She resigns from teaching at SDB and joins American Expeditionary Force Siberia as a Red Cross nurse during the Russian Civil War.

SDB student Pedro Santos enters CSD.

1920: On October 3, Delight's mother Alice dies in Manila.

1923: On January 16, Delight departs from Manila for San Francisco, upon her doctor's orders.

She enrolls SDB students Bernardo Cuengco and Lester Naftaly at CSD.

In June, SDB again moves to its fourth and permanent location on F.B. Harrison Street in Pasay City in Manila.

In October, her father Charles returns to join her in Palo Alto, California, from Manila after resigning from SDB.

1924: She teaches a lipreading class at Gough School for the Oral Deaf in San Francisco.

1925: Bernardo Cuengco graduates from CSD.

1928: In September, Delight inaugurates special classes for hard of hearing children at Berkeley Public Schools (BPS) in Berkeley, California.

1929: On March 8, she tests more than one hundred children using an audiometer.

1931: Lester Naftaly graduates from CSD and enrolls at Gallaudet College.

1932: Delight is officially commended for devising an audiological testing method by an audiometer inventor.

She sees Ronald Hirano as an infant in a cradle in Berkeley, California, when his parents visit her for consultation.

1933: On October 16, her father Charles dies in Berkeley, California.

1934: She consults with the parents of Jeanette Davis and recommends that they enroll her at CSD.

1937: She drives five-year-old Ronald to Vallejo, consults with the parents of Daniel Lynch, and recommends they enroll Daniel at CSD.

1938: She finds George Attletweed in a Berkeley public school and recommends that he be enrolled at CSD.

George, Jeanette and Ronald enroll at CSD.

1939: Daniel enters CSD.

1942: In April, she takes over the guardianship of Ronald just before the forced evacuation of his entire family along with 120,000 Japanese-Americans from the Pacific Coast to internment camps.

In May, she drives Ronald to visit his family interned at an assembly camp at Tanforan Racetrack in San Bruno, California.

1943: She interprets the negotiations to purchase a clubhouse in Oakland, California, for East Bay Club for the Deaf.

1944: She takes Ronald to visit his family at an internment camp in Topaz, Utah.

1947: George graduates from CSD and enters Gallaudet College.

1949: Delight retires from Berkeley Public Schools at the mandatory age of sixty-five years.

She is employed by Hearing Center of Metropolitan Los Angeles (HCMLA) in Los Angeles, California.

She manages California Home for the Aged Deaf on Menlo Avenue in Los Angeles.

She teaches summer audiological classes at College (now University) of Pacific in Stockton, California.

1952: Jeanette and Ronald graduate from CSD. She gets married, and he enrolls at Gallaudet College.

1953: Daniel graduates from CSD and enrolls at Gallaudet College.

1955: On June 4, Delight receives an honorary doctorate from Gallaudet College.

1958: She welcomes a visit from Richard West, president of Philippine Association of the Deaf (PAD), in Berkeley, California.

1959: She retires from HCMLA at the age of seventy-five.

1961: On September 7, she arrives at Manila for the first time in thirty-eight years, with some three hundred attendees welcoming her. Her visit is highly publicized in major newspapers.

She is showered with awards and honors at numerous banquets. On December 22, a historical marker at SDB is unveiled in her honor.

Delight extends her stay in the Philippines from December to March 1962 upon the alumni's request.

1962: On March 4, she is honored at a farewell banquet by School of the Deaf Alumni Association.

She leaves Manila for a six-week tour visiting deaf and blind schools in Asia and Europe, as provided by the Tourism of the Philippine Board of Travel and Tourists.

1964: On October 9, she dies at age eighty-one in Berkeley, California, and is buried in a family plot at Five Corners Cemetery in Milfordton Township, Ohio.

2007: On January 19, the unveiling ceremony of a centennial historical marker at PSD launches the year-long Centennial Celebration, and a commemorative postage stamp is presented in honor of the PSD's 100th anniversary.

On December 1-9 during the closing of the Centennial Celebration at PSD, Ronald gives a tribute to his foster mother Delight and, on behalf of CSD Supt. Henry Klopping, Stanley Smith presents a CSD history book to PSD Principal Yolanda Capulong.

**The Parent-Teacher Association of
School for the Deaf and the Blind**
September 17, 1961

Ronald Hirano, guest speaker

Presenting a fundraising speech
for the PSD's Centennial Celebration
at Gallaudet University in
Washington, DC, on April 21, 2007

About the Author

Roland James

Ronald Hirano, general chairperson

Giving a welcome speech at the DSA conference
in San Francisco on August 31, 2005

About the Author

Writing a book is a challenge, especially for novices like Ronald Hirano. Although he has written articles and stories since his high school days at the California School for the Deaf (CSD) in Berkeley, this book is so unique that he has a personal connection to its subject and that it is his first book.

The eldest of four boys and two girls, Ronald was born Deaf. His brother Robert is also hard of hearing. Before the sixth child's birth in 1947, his parents intended to name the baby Delight Rice. But the baby was a male and they named him Gordon Rice instead. His father, James S. Hirano, was born in Japan. Before the war, he owned a supermarket in Oakland. Afterwards, he owned an import and wholesale business specializing in oriental antiques and furniture. His mother, Mary S. Hirano, was born in San Francisco of Japanese ancestry, and was a homemaker and a world traveler.

After his 1952 graduation from CSD, Ronald earned an associate's degree from Gallaudet College in 1955 and then a bachelor's degree from San Francisco State University in 1984. He has always been very actively involved with the deaf community, serving as a member and officer of the boards of DEAF Media, Deaf Counseling, Advocacy & Referral Agency (DCARA), Bay Area Coalition of Deaf Senior Citizens (BACDSC), Deaf Seniors of America (DSA), Bay Area Asian Deaf Association (BAADA), and California School for the Deaf Alumni Association (CSDAA). For six years, he was treasurer for the DSA national board, and chaired the 8th Biennial DSA Conference in San Francisco in 2005. He was treasurer for the Filipino-American fundraising committee as well as auditor for the native committee for the Centennial Celebration of PSD in Pasay City, Philippines in 2007. He is currently the vice president of CSDAA.

Ronald's next book will be an autobiography.

School for the Deaf and the Blind
Pasay, Metro Manila

Appendix

SCHOOL FOR THE DEAF AND THE BLIND
(1907)

PIONEER SCHOOL FOR THE HANDICAPPED IN THE PHILIPPINES. PLANNED BY DR. DAVID P. BARROWS, DIRECTOR OF EDUCATION; ORGANIZED BY MISS DELIA DELIGHT RICE, PRINCIPAL TEACHER (1907 - 1923). IT WAS ESTABLISHED IN THE CITY OF MANILA WHERE IT REMAINED UNTIL IT WAS TRANSFERRED TO ITS PRESENT SITE IN PASAY CITY, JUNE 1923.

LEADING INSTITUTION FOR THE EDUCATION OF THE DEAF AND THE BLIND IN THE PHILIPPINES.

Appendix

List of SDB and PSD Principals and Officers-in-Charge:

Delight Rice, Principal, 1907-1923

Julia Hayes, Principal, 1923-1936

Lucretia Belting, Principal, 1936-1940

Elvira Llanes, Officer-in-Charge, 1940-1941

Florenco Castro, Officer-in-Charge, 1941

Maria V. Francisco, Principal, 1946-1960

Francisco C. Tan, Officer-in-Charge, 1960

Sergia T. Esguerra, Special Schools Principal, 1960-1963

Felicidad P. Vinluan, Special Schools Principal, 1963-1971

Rosario F. Castro, Special Schools Principal, 1972-1975

Aurora B. Ramirez, Officer-in-Charge, 1974

Alfonso P. Agringo, Officer-in-Charge, 1974-1975

Virginia C. Gorospe, Officer-in-Charge, 1975

Isabel L. Leuterio, Officer-in-Charge, 1976-1977

Hermogenes C. Bundac, Special Schools Principal II, 1977-1985

Gerardo A. Consolacion, Officer-in-Charge, 1986-1987

Yolanda T. Capulong, Officer-in-Charge, 1987
and Special Schools Principal II, 1987-Present

San Francisco ⊙
Los Angeles ⊙

United States of America

⊙ Washington

Atlantic Ocean

Pacific Ocean

Map of the World

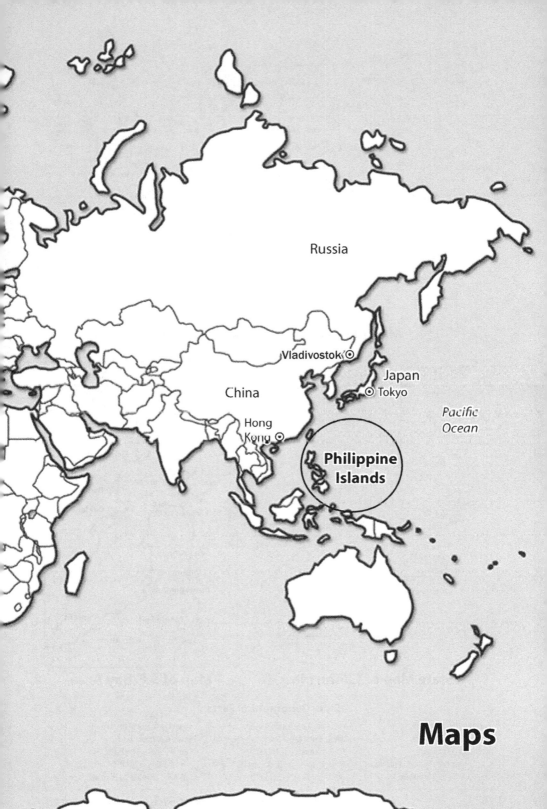

Russia

Vladivostok ⊙

China

Japan
⊙ Tokyo

Pacific
Ocean

Hong
Kong ⊙

**Philippine
Islands**

Maps

Map of the United States of America

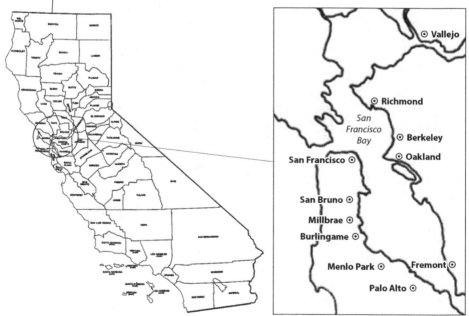

State Map of California

Map of S.F. Bay Area

State Geographical Facts

Total area: 163,896 sq. mi.
Counties: 58   Cities: 460
Population: 38 million,
                most populous in the U.S.
Economy: 9th largest in the world

Agriculture: Largest in the nation
Tallest, largest and oldest trees in the world:
    Coast redwoods – 379 ft. tall
    Giant sequoias – 36 ft. dia. and 113 ft. girth
    Bristlecone pines – Over 5,000 years old

Highest and lowest points
in the contiguous U.S.A.:
    Mt. Whitney –14,505 ft.
    Death Valley – 282 ft. below sea level
    85 miles separate these points

The Life Story of Mother Delight Rice and Her Children

State Map of Ohio

Map of Central Ohio

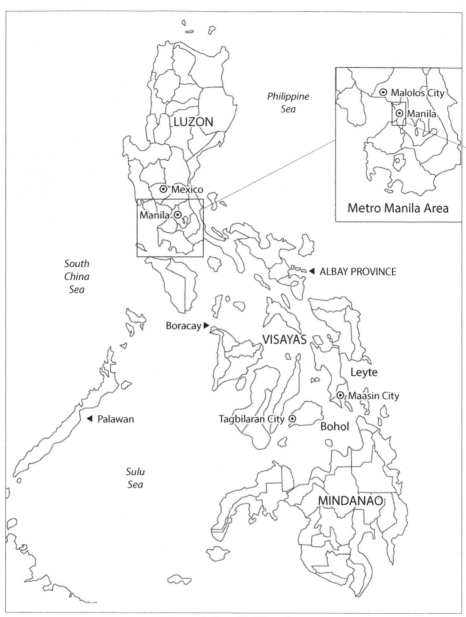

Map of the Philippines

Geographical Facts

Islands: 7,107
Paradise islands:
  Boracay
  Palawan
Total area: 115,831 sq.mi.
  Approx. size of Arizona

Regions: 17
Provinces: 80
Cities: 138
Population:
  98 million
Metro Manila
  21 million

Official languages:
  Filipino and English
Religions:
  Roman Catholics: 81%
  Other Christians: 12%
  Muslims: 5%
  Others: 2%

The Life Story of Mother Delight Rice and Her Children

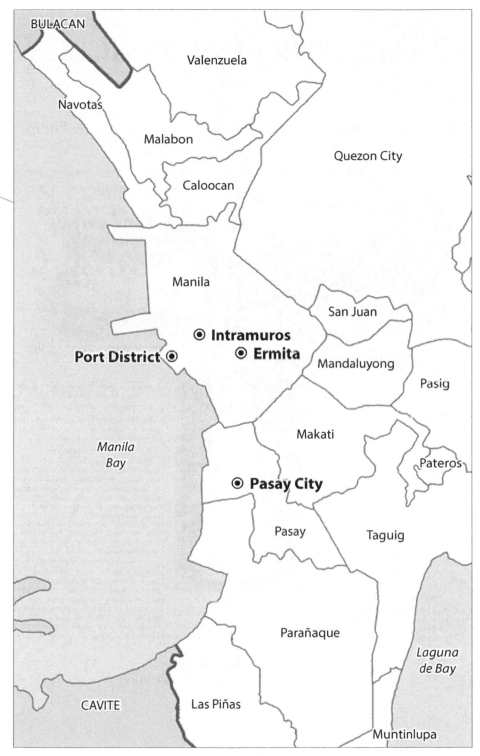

BULACAN

Valenzuela

Navotas

Malabon

Quezon City

Caloocan

Manila

San Juan

⦿ **Intramuros**

Port District ⦿ ⦿ **Ermita**

Mandaluyong

Pasig

Makati

Manila
Bay

Pateros

⦿ **Pasay City**

Pasay

Taguig

Parañaque

Laguna
de Bay

CAVITE

Las Piñas

Muntinlupa

Map of Metro Manila

THE OHIO CHRONICLE.

— *Published by and for the State School for the Deaf.* —

VOLUME XLI.   COLUMBUS, OHIO, SATURDAY, FEBRUARY 27, 1909.

Miss Delight Rice, the School She Founded in the Philippines, and Some of Her Pupils

Article and Illustrations from the Columbus Evening Dispatch.

Manila Institute for the Deaf and Dumb.

MISS RICE.

A group of Miss Rice's pupils at the Manila Institute.

Miss Delight Rice, who was for three years teacher of a class of deaf and blind pupils at the Wisconsin School for the Deaf, and who is known in Columbus through her work in teaching John P. Riley, a deaf, dumb and blind boy, who is a pupil at the Ohio Institute for the Deaf, is now in the Philippine Islands in charge of a school for the Deaf at Manila.

Miss Rice received an appointment as teacher of the deaf in the Philippines from the United States government, and journeyed to Manila to take up her work. Arriving there she found there was no such school and that no preparations whatever had been made for any such work.

MADE HER OWN SCHOOL.

Miss Rice started to work, nevertheless. She found a deaf and dumb girl and commenced to teach her. In her spare time she traveled over the Philipines, from one end to the other, usually alone, hunting the deaf and dumb, and finally her class grew so large that the establishment of a school became a necessity.

WAS MADE PRINCIPAL.

She established the school under the direction of Uncle Sam, and was made principal, but managed to continue her travels, interesting parents in her work, until finally the class grew so large that an assistant was necessary. On application to Washington for help the assistant was furnished, and the Manila Institute for the Deaf is now quite an important school.

A COMPETENT TEACHER.

Miss Rice's work while in Columbus attracted general attention. She is a most competent instructor, and doubtless her good work will be extended in the Philippines until the education of the deaf and dumb is recognized as a fixed part of the educational system of the islands.

The Ohio Chronicle

An Ohio School for the Deaf Publication

Silent Worker.

"The foundation of every State is the education of its youth."—Dionysius.

| VOL. XXI NO. 8 | TRENTON, N. J., MAY, 1909. | 5 CENTS A COPY |

Miss Rice, the School She Founded in the Philippines, and Some of Her Pupils

MANILA INSTITUTE FOR THE DEAF AND DUMB.

A GROUP OF MISS RICE'S PUPILS AT THE MANILA INSTITUTE.

MISS DELIGHT RICE, who was for three years teacher of a class of deaf and blind pupils at the Wisconsin School for the Deaf, and who is known in Columbus through her work in teaching John P. Riley, a deaf, dumb and blind boy, who is a pupil at the Ohio Institute for the Deaf, is now in the Philippine Islands in charge of a school for the Deaf at Manila.

Miss Rice received an appointment as teacher of the deaf in the Philippines from the United States government, and journeyed to Manila to take up her work. Arriving there she found there was no such school and that no preparations whatever had been made for any such work.

MADE HER OWN SCHOOL

Miss Rice started to work, nevertheless. She found a deaf and dumb girl and commenced to teach her. In her spare time she traveled over the Philippines from one end to the other, usually alone, hunting for the deaf and dumb, and finally her class grew so large that the establishment of a school became a necessity.

WAS MADE PRINCIPAL

She established the school under the direction of Uncle Sam, and was made principal, but managed to continue her travels, interesting parents in her work, until finally the class grew so large that an assistant was necessary. On application to Washington for help the assistant was furnished, and the Manila Institute for the Deaf is now quite an important school.

A COMPETENT TEACHER

Miss Rice's work while in Columbus attracted general attention. She is a most

MISS DELIGHT RICE

competent instructor, and doubtless her good work will be extended in the Philippines until the education of the deaf and dumb is recognized as a fixed part of the educational system of the islands.

The article above was taken from the *Columbus Evening Dispatch.*

One of the pictures shows Miss Rice

guarded by United States soldiers and a U. S. army wagon she traveled some distance in. On all trips over the Island after the deaf children, she was guarded by United States soldiers. The bracelet seen on her arm was presented by a Moro, so ferocious no white woman had courage to go very near. She got more information through means of signs to the Moros than others in the party got through an interpreter, which goes far to prove that the sign-language is as perfect a universal language as it is possible to devise.

Miss Rice has one year more under her contract. Her present school term closed April 1st, and on April 3d she left for China to spend the vacation.

Miss Rice's work among the deaf and blind, her extreme youth when she took up that work, and handling a class of three to four of these unfortunate children in Wisconsin; her work with John Porter Riley in the State School for the Deaf in Columbus; the passing of the United States government examination for the appointment to teach the deaf in the Philippines; her long trip alone; her struggle and trips over the Island to get the parents to *allow* their deaf children to attend school, is something not many young girls could have carried out alone. She established the school and has been Superintendent, Principal, teacher, matron, mother, nurse, steward, cook and even dish-washer when cholera was so near the building as to make it unsafe for the help to go and come. In fact, at one time she fired the cook for unsanitary reasons and took her place temporarily. Her work in the cause of deaf-mute education deserves all the encouragement it is possible to give her.

The Silent Worker
A National Publication

Bibliography

AFTER 38 YEARS' ABSENCE

Founder Of School For Deaf And Blind Returns To Be With Her Old Friends

By JOEL SON. PANTI

Last Sept. 7 was a feast day for some 300 students and alumni of the School For Deaf and Blind of Pasay City. The occasion was the arrival of Dr. Delight Rice, founder and first principal of the school.

The 63-year-old philanthropist, who founded the school in 1907, returned after 38 years of absence to visit her friends, students, alumni and "children" of the School For Deaf and Blind.

"I'm indeed very happy to see again my old friends in your country. I'm already old and all I wanted all these years is to be with them," she said.

Dr. Rice spent her best years in the Philippines and she demonstrated most effectively the advantages of educating the handicapped, specially the deaf and the blind.

"I believe that these unfortunates will be just as useful as any normal person if they are given the chance to develop their individual skill," she explained.

She started the first school for the handicapped here with a handful of pupils. It grew into a progressive institution as the years went by.

The school started in a small house in Manila. In 1923, it was moved to a large concrete building on the Bay of Pasco. It flourished during the years when Leonard Wood was the governor general, who was also instrumental in the school's initial success.

When World War II broke out, the school was closed. However, shortly after the U.S. granted the Philippines the right to govern herself, it was reopened as a day

DR. DELIGHT RICE is shown being greeted by well-wishers upon arrival at the International airport recently.

school. There were only 120 deaf pupils and 16 blind children enrolled. But in 1950 the number increased.

The school offers ten years of instruction broken down into six years elementary and four years of high school.

Seven years later, there was some improvement. Dormitories were reopened and the enrollment of blind students increased to 37.

To augment the school training facilities, a pilot and adjustment training center was opened in February, 1957. This facility, which is now a small impossing plant, is now operating under the Philippine Office of Vocational Rehabilitation (Cubao, Quezon City) with the American Foundation for Overseas Blind providing the services of a consultant and funds and equipment.

The center is offering a full program of training and work experience for more than 60 blind clients. These clients are now serving the Far East region as a teaching and demonstrating unit for preparing instructors for other countries such as India, Free China, Pakistan, Vietnam and Japan.

With the establishment of rehabilitation services in Manila, provincial commissions, at least in embryo, have also commenced to operate in Zamboanga City, Baguio City and Cebu City.

All these are now possible because of the pioneering spirit of Dr. Rice. Aside from the school and rehabilitation centers duly registered organizations, dedicated to the uplift of the handicapped have also been formed by civic-spirited groups.

These organizations are: Foundation of the Blind of the Philippines, Inc.; United Blind Association, Inc.; Philippine Association for the Sightless, Inc.; Blind Association of the Philippines, Inc.; Philippine Pathfinder For the Blind; Philippine Blind, Deaf, Dumb and Crippled Association, and others.

Now more than 300 students coming from all parts of the country enjoy the fruits which Dr. Delight Rice toiled for. Some of these met her at the airport. She said she could not help but shed tears when welcomers hugged and greeted her with sign languages.

Graduates of the school are now employed in trade or business firms or engaged in other professions.

She said that her stay here would be indefinite. She indicated, however, she might even spend Christmas here with her "children."

Bibliography

BOOKS

Class of 1960. *1860-1960 Centennial, California School for the Deaf Berkeley*. Berkeley: California School for the Deaf, 1960. Print.

Datuin, Gregorio M. *People of the Silent World*. Manila, Philippines: Philippine Association of the Deaf, 1976. Print.

Forbes, William Cameron. "The success of the institution." *The Philippine Islands, Vol. 1*. Boston: Houghton Mifflin, 1928. 459-60. Print.

Hill Jr., N.N. "Rice and Hawkins families in Milfordton Township." *History of Knox County, Ohio*. Mount Vernon, Ohio: A. A. Graham, 1881. 513-19. Print.

Howe, Henry. "The Institution for the Education of the Deaf and Dumb." *Historical Collections of Ohio, Franklin County*. Cincinnati: The State of Ohio, 1902. 636-39. Print.

Norton, Kenneth. *The Deaf at Work*. Berkeley: California School for the Deaf, 1967. Print.

—. *The Eagle Soars to Enlightenment*. Fremont: California School for the Deaf, 2001. 362-63. Print.

Perkins, Eugene. *Malarañang Residence of the Governor-General: A Historical Resume of the Palace under Spanish and American Sovereignty in the Philippines*. Manila, Philippines: Philippine Education Company, 1922. Print.

Rianda, Eugene. *California School for the Deaf Album of Graduates 1871-2010*. Fremont: California School for the Deaf, 2010. Print.

—. *Memories of the California School for the Deaf Berkeley/Fremont Alumni*. Fremont: California School for the Deaf Alumni Association, 1995. Print.

Robinson, Warren. *A Suggestive Manual for the Use of Parents and Pupils*. Delavan: Wisconsin School for the Deaf, 1904. Print.

Roe, W. R. *Peeps into the Deaf World*. Derby and London, England: Bemrose & Sons Limited, 1917. 294-95. Print.

Wade, William. *A Monograph: The Blind-Deaf*. Indianapolis: Hecker Brothers 1904. 9-12 and 112. Print.

Winzer, Margaret A. "Chapter IV Isolated to Be Educated: Delia Delight Rice's Contribution to the Growth of SPED in the Philippines." *The History of Special Education: From Isolation to Integration*. Washington, DC: Gallaudet University Press, 1993. 51-83. Print.

NEWSPAPERS AND PERIODICALS

Argila, Carl A. "Land of the Morning, Child of the Sun Returning." *Deaf American*
Dec. 1970: 5-7. Print.

—. "The SAID in the Philippines." *Deaf American* Mar. 1975: 12-14. Print.

"Be Sure Your Child Can Hear." *Van Nuys News* 7 Sept. 1950: 48. Print.

"Berkeley Education Board Helps Deaf." *Oakland Tribune* 9 July 1935: 5. Web.
24 June 2012.

"Berkeley Votes New Class for Defective." *Oakland Tribune* 18 Sept. 1928: 23.
Web. 24 June 2012.

"The CAD Convention." *California News* Oct. 1950: 9. Print.

"Charles Merrick Rice." *California News* 25 Oct. 1933: 41. Print.

"Closing Exercises: C.M. Rice." *Ohio Chronicle* 13 June 1879. Print.

Cuengco, Bernardo. "An Autobiographical Sketch by Bernardo Cuengco."
California News Sept. 1923: 1-3. Print.

"Deaf and Dumb Institute." *Piqua Leader Dispatch* 23 Sept. 1907: 7. Print.

"A Deaf Philippino." *Silent Worker* Jan. 1920: 23. Print.

"Deaf Philippino in California School." *Ohio Chronicle* 25 Oct. 1919. Print.

"Death of Mrs. Alice I. Rice." *Ohio Chronicle* 15 May 1920. Print.

"Death of Mrs. Charles M. Rice of Manila." *Oakland Tribune* 29 May 1920: 14.
Web. 24 June 2012.

"Death of Mrs. Charles M. Rice of Manila." *Oakland Tribune* 7 June 1920: 6.
Web. 24 June 2012.

"Deaths – Rice, Delight in Berkeley." *Oakland Tribune* 10 Oct. 1964: 22. Web.
24 June 2012.

"Deaths – Rice, Percy E. in Oakland." *Oakland Tribune* 2 Apr. 1960: 35. Web.
24 June 2012.

"Defective Speech Classes Now Exist in 80 U.S. Cities." *Oakland Tribune*
16 Sept. 1931: 12. Web. 24 June 2012.

"Delight Rice Appointed as Teacher in the Philippines." *American Annals of
the Deaf* 52 (1907): 296. Print.

"Delight Rice Going to the Philippines." *Ohio Chronicle* 6 Apr. 1907. Print.

"Delight Rice Resigned from Wisconsin School for the Deaf." *American Annals of
the Deaf* 50 (1905): 398. Print.

"Delight Rice's New Employment at WSD." The Picture Gallery. *Wisconsin Times*
1 Oct. 1903. Print.

"Delight Rice's Visit in the Philippines." *Manila Free Press* [Manila, Philippines]
5 Sept. 1961. Print.

"Demonstration." *Oakland Tribune* 18 Mar. 1945: 40. Web. 24 June 2012.

D'Estrella, T. "Charles Rice's Return Home from the Philippines." *California News*
Nov. 1923: 38. Print.

—. "Delight Rice Nearly Overboard." *California News* Mar. 1923: 102. Print.

—. "Gilbert Brink was the Boys' Dormitory Supervisor." *California News* May 1909: 7. Print.

—. "Lester Naftaly's 'Stunt' Flying." *California News* 20 Mar. 1929: 149-50. Print.

—. "Miss Lagman." *California News* Apr. 1910: 5. Print.

—. "Miss Rice has been Progressing Satisfactorily." *California News* May 1909: 7. Print.

—. "Mrs. Charles Rice and Her Two Sons." *California News* Dec. 1910: 6. Print.

—. "Paula Felizardo Returned to Manila." *California News* 15 May 1914: 280. Print.

—. "Pedro Santos Did Not Enter Gallaudet College." *California News* Sept. 1922: 12-13. Print.

"Dr. Delight Rice." *California News* Nov. 1964: 11. Print.

"Dr. Rice Visits Philippine Deaf, Blind." *Silent Worker* Oct. 1961: 6. Print.

"East Bay Club for the Deaf." *Oakland Tribune* 5 Sept. 1946: 17. Web. 24 June 2012.

"East Bay Club Improves Quarters." *California News* Oct. 1946: 10. Print.

"Education in the Philippines." *American Annals of the Deaf* 52 (1907): 208. Print.

"Efforts in the Philippines." *Deaf American* Dec. 1971: 2. Print.

8th Annual Report of the Director of Education for the fiscal year July 1, 1907 to June 30, 1908. Manila: Bureau of Printing, 1908. Print.

"Establishment of WRA Centers Mistake—Myer." *Tulean Dispatch Daily* 28 May 1943: 1. Print.

15th Annual Report of the Director of Education for the fiscal year January 1, 1914 to December 31, 1914. Manila: Bureau of Printing, 1914. Print.

"The Filipino School Gives an Exhibition." *Ohio Chronicle* 17 Feb. 1912. Print.

"Freed at Santo Tomas." *California News* Mar. 1945: 74. Print.

"From Delight Rice." *Ohio Chronicle* 15 Feb. 1908. Print.

"From the Philippines." *Silent Worker* Dec. 1911: 43-44. Print.

"From the Philippines by Alice Rice." *Ohio Chronicle* 23 Sept. 1911. Print.

"Good Hearing Found Common." *Oakland Tribune* 19 June 1933: 20. Web. 24 June 2012.

"Handicapped Pupils to Get Special Aid." *Berkeley Daily Gazette* 18 Sept. 1928: 1+. Web. 24 June 2012.

"Helen Keller School Holds Party Last Sat." *Tulean Dispatch Daily* 12 Aug. 1943: 1. Print.

"Helen Keller Sends Message to Handicapped Student Here." *Tulean Dispatch Daily* 13 August 1943: 2. Print.

Hirano, Ronald. "A Story from the Philippine Islands." *California News* Oct. 1945: 24. Print.

"Honors Pour on Dr. Delight Rice." *Silent Worker* Feb. 1962: 3. Print.

"Human Sacrifice of Deaf Boy." *Silent Worker* July 1909: 4. Print.

"The Importance of Teaching the Blind-Deaf to Work." *American Annals of the Deaf* 50 (1905): 392-96. Print.

"Jealousy Cause of Stammering." *Piqua Leader Dispatch* 19 Feb. 1932: 3. Print.

"The last census of the Philippines." *Silent Worker* Nov. 1907: 17. Print.
"A letter from the Philippine Islands." *Silent Worker* Nov. 1919: 11. Print.
"Letter from the Philippines by Alice Rice." *Ohio Chronicle* 12 Oct. 1912. Print.
"Letter from the Philippines by Delight Rice." *Ohio Chronicle* 22 May 1909. Print.
Lindholm, Toivo. "The Deaf of the Philippines." *Silent Worker* Feb. 1959: 3-4. Print.

Mallari, Perry Gil S. "A Century of Absolute Commitment." *Manila Times* [Manila, Philippines] 25 Feb. 2007. Web.
"The Manila School." *Ohio Chronicle* 3 April 1909. Print.
"The Manila School." *Silent Worker* June 1914: 10+. Print.
"Married: Rice-Gregg." *Ohio Chronicle* 18 Sept. 1880. Print.
"Married in Hong Kong on Feb. 7, 1911." *Silent Worker* Oct. 1911: 17. Print.
"Married to R.G. Webber and Quotation on New School." *American Annals of the Deaf* 56 (1911): 549. Print.
Meyers, Wildey. "Delight Rice Honored." *California News* 12 Dec. 1941: 65. Print.
"Miss Delight Rice." *Silent Worker* Jan. 1908: 17. Print.
"Miss Delight Rice." *Silent Worker* Feb. 1908. 17. Print.
"Miss Delight Rice, a Teacher of a Deaf-Blind Boy." *Silent Worker* June 1907: 3. Print.
"Miss Delight Rice, the School She Founded." *Ohio Chronicle* 27 Feb. 1909. Print.
"Miss Delight Rice's Beautiful Signs." *Silent Worker* July 1907: 17. Print.
"Miss Paula Pecson Appointed to be a Native Teacher." *American Annals of the Deaf* 55 (1910): 202. Print.
"Miss Rice and Her Pupils." *Ohio Chronicle* 29 Sept. 1906. Print.
"Miss Rice, the School She Founded in the Philippines." *Silent Worker* May 1909: 1-2. Print.
"Miss Rice to Venture into the Interior of Philippines." *Ohio Chronicle* 7 Dec. 1907. Print.
"Moved to a Former Medical College." *American Annals of the Deaf* 56 (1911): 106. Print.
"Mrs. D. Rice Webber Goes to Siberia as Nurse." *Ohio Chronicle* 8 Mar. 1919. Print.
"Mrs. Webber is Spending Some Months in Southern California." *Silent Worker* Apr. 1914: 7-8. Print.

"A New Clubhouse." Editorial. *California News* Jan. 1944: 59. Print.
"New Pasay School." *American Annals of the Deaf* 68 (1923): 87. Print.
"New Pasay School Cost." *American Annals of the Deaf* 66.5 (1921): 489. Print.
"The New School for the Deaf." *Silent Worker* Dec. 1908: 17. Print.

"Our Deaf-Blind Students and Teacher." *Wisconsin Times* 7 Apr. 1904: 1. Print.

"The Philippine School." *Ohio Chronicle* 7 Nov. 1908. Print.
"The Philippine School." *Ohio Chronicle* 5 Nov. 1910. Print.
"The Philippine School at Manila." *Silent Worker* Jan. 1911: 17. Print.
"Philippine School in Charge of Deaf Principal." *Silent Worker* July 1920: 7. Print.
"Plans to Organize Education Program for Handicapped Made."
    Tulean Dispatch Daily 22 May 1943: 1. Print.

"Red Cross Nurse to Siberia." *American Annals of the Deaf* 64 (1919): 78. Print.
"Retirement Photo." *Oakland Tribune* 22 May 1949: 22. Web. 24 June 2012.
Rice, Charles. "The Philippine School for the Deaf and the Blind." *Silent Worker*
    Jan. 1921: 11+. Print.
Rice, Delight. "The School for the Deaf and the Blind." *The Philippine Review* 1.9
    July-Sept. 1916: 42-43. Print.
"R.R. Lagman and Delight Rice in the PI Hinterland." *California News* Sept. 1909:
    6. Print.

"Salary of Miss Delight Rice—$2,460 Per Annum." *Berkeley Daily Gazette*
    16 Oct. 1928: 20. Web. 24 June 2012.
"Sale of Filipinos." *Silent Worker* July 1910: 15. Print.
Santos, Pedro C. "Alice I. Rice Died in the Philippines." *California News*
    May 1920: 160-61. Print.
"School for Deaf Founder Here." *Manila Times* [Manila, Philippines] 8 Sept. 1961.
    Print.
"The School for the Deaf in Manila." *Silent Worker* Feb. 1911: 17. Print.
"The School of the Deaf in the Philippines." *Ohio Chronicle* 16 Nov. 1907. Print.
"School Supported by Government." *American Annals of the Deaf* 53 (1908):
    173-74. Print.
"Siberia and Engaged to Army Officer." *California News* Nov. 1919: 30-31. Print.
"Some Parents Are so Clever." *Silent Worker* Dec. 1919: 12. Print.
Son Panti, Joel. "Founder of School for Deaf and Blind Returns to Be with Her
    Old Friends." *Manila Bulletin* [Manila, Philippines] 16 Sept. 1961. Print.
"Speech on Topaz Camp Visit." *Oakland Tribune* 1 Dec. 1944: 21. Web.
    24 June 2012.
"Suiting the Occasion." *Silent Worker* Jan. 1921: 18. Print.
"Survey." *Oakland Tribune* 17 Oct. 1928: 13. Web. 24 June 2012.

"Test Hearing of Children." *Oakland Tribune* 20 Dec. 1932: 17. Web.
    24 June 2012.
"Tests on Hearing." *Berkeley Daily Gazette* 9 Mar. 1929: 3. Web. 24 June 2012.
"12 Schools Are Given Courses in Lip Reading." *Berkeley Daily Gazette*
    2 May 1930: 13. Web. 24 June 2012.
"22 pupils as of 11-10-1908." *American Annals of the Deaf* 54 (1909): 193. Print.

"Visited Milford Township." *Mt. Vernon News* 30 June 1955. Print.

"Wisconsin's Helen Kellers." *Wisconsin Times* 26 Nov. 1904. Print.
"With the Silent Workers." *Silent Worker* Oct. 1914: 1-3. Print.

PAPERS

"Alumni Cards." 1914. MS. Archival collection of Gallaudet University Archives.
    Archivist Michael Olson e-mailed to the author. 26 Dec. 2009.
Argila, Carl A. *The Philippine National School for the Deaf.* Nov. 1973. MS.
    Personal collection of Anita Ner, handed to the author. 9 Aug. 2011.
Attletweed, George. Collected papers. 1930-1990. TS. Personal collection of
    Bernadette Attletweed, e-mailed to the author. 7 May 2012.

"Charles 'Buddy' Sutton Rice." Collected papers. 1973. TS. Genealogical
    collection of Ancestry.com. Joyce Ingraham e-mailed to the author.
    11 Jan. 2012.
"Charles Merrick Rice." Collected papers. 1906 or 1907. TS. Genealogical
    collection of Ancestry.com. Joyce Ingraham e-mailed to the author.
    10 Jan. 2012.
"Class of 1874 Graduation Program." June 16, 1874. Collected papers. 1874. TS.
    Archival collection of Ohio School for the Deaf Library.
    Librarian Nancy Boone e-mailed to the author. 2012.
"Commencement Exercises of the Twenty-fourth Graduating Class." 1903. TS.
    Personal collection of the author.
Cuengco, Bernardo. Collected papers. 1904-1978. TS. Personal collection of
    Maria Banez, mailed to the author. 18 Oct. 2006.

Daviton, Jeanette Davis. Collected papers. 1932-2012. TS. Personal collection
    of Jeanette Davis Daviton. Laura Daviton e-mailed to the author.
    26 Jan. 2012.
"Decree of Divorce." 1915. TS. Personal collection of the author.
"Delia Gregg and Cecelia Delight Alexander." Collected papers. 1829-1896. TS.
    Genealogical collection of Ancestry.com. Joyce Ingraham e-mailed to the
    author. 6 Jan. 2012.
"Delight Rice." Collected papers. 1888-2012. TS. Genealogical collection of
    Ancestry.com. Joyce Ingraham e-mailed to the author. 7 Jan. 2012.
"Delight Rice and Eva Halliday." Illustration. 1904. TS. Archival collection of
    Harvard University, Library of the Graduate School of Education.
    Thomas Bull mailed to the author. 10 Jan. 2006.

"Emergency Passport Application." Illustration. 1912-1920. TS. Genealogical
    collection of Ancestry.com. Joyce Ingraham e-mailed to the author.
    12 Feb. 2011.

Hanson, Agatha Tiegel. Letter to Leonard Elstad, President of Gallaudet College.
    10 Oct. 1954. MS. Archival collection of Gallaudet University Archives.
    Thomas Bull mailed to the author. 10 Jan. 2006.

"Harris Hawkins and Phebe Lowell." Collected papers. 1787-1856. TS. Genealogical collection of Ancestry.com. Joyce Ingraham e-mailed to the author. 16 Dec. 2011.

Inciong, Dr. Teresita G. *The Development of Welfare and Education for Children with Mental Retardation.* Seisa University. Hokkaido, Japan. 9-10 July 2005. Paper presentation.

"Julia Hayes." Collected papers. 1875. TS. Genealogical collection of Ancestry.com. Joyce Ingraham e-mailed to the author. 28 May 2012.

"Lester Naftaly." Collected papers. 1936. MS. Archival collection of Gallaudet University Archives. Archivist Michael Olson e-mailed to the author. 2 Feb. 2011.

"List of SDB and PSD Principals and Officers-in-Charge." 1907-2012. TS. Archival collection of Philippine School for the Deaf Library. Renato Cruz e-mailed to the author. 15 June 2012.

Lynch, Daniel. Collected papers. 1937-2012. TS. Personal collection of Daniel Lynch, e-mailed to the author. 12 May 2012.

"Marriage Record No. 3114 of Charles M. Rice and Alice I. Gregg on July 15, 1880." Illustration. Archival collection of Gallaudet University Archives. Archivist Michael Olson e-mailed to the author. 8 Apr. 2012.

Martinez, Liza B. and Rafaelito M. Abat. *The History of Sign Language in the Philippines Piecing Together the Puzzle.* 2006. TS. Web.

"1918 Manila Map." Illustration. 1918. MS. Archival collection of Ateneo de Manila University, Rizal Library, American Historical Collection. Renato Cruz e-mailed to the author. 3 Nov. 2011.

"Ohio School for the Deaf - 1874." Collected papers. 1874. TS. Archival collection of Ohio School for the Deaf Library. Richard Hubner e-mailed to the author. 9 Jan. 2012.

Parsons, Frances. "Delight Rice." N.d. TS. Personal collection of the author.

"Pedro C. Santos." Collected papers. 1920-1922. MS. Archival collection of Gallaudet University Archives. Archivist Michael Olson e-mailed to the author. 2 Feb. 2011.

"Percy Eugene Rice." Collected papers. 1917. TS. Genealogical collection of Ancestry.com. Joyce Ingraham e-mailed to the author. 17 Jan. 2012.

"Ralph Grant Webber of Maine." Collected papers. 1911-1920. TS. Candice Critchfield e-mailed to the author. 8 May 2010.

Ramello, Regino. Letter to Delight Rice. Collected papers. 1945. MS. Personal collection of the author.

Rice. Collected papers. 1808-1964. MS. Archival collection of Delaware County Genealogical Society. Archivist Millie Barnhart mailed to the author. 19 Mar. 2012.

Rice, Charles Merrick. Collected letters of Charles Merrick Rice. 1874/1879.
MS. Archival collection of Gallaudet University Archives.
Archivist Michael Olson mailed to the author. 15 Feb. 2011.

Rice, Delight. Collected papers. 1883-1964. MS. Personal collection of the
author.

—. Collected letters of Delight Rice. 1901 and 1907. MS. Archival collection of
Gallaudet University Archives. Archivist Michael Olson mailed to
the author. 15 Feb. 2011.

—. "Diary." Collected papers. 1907-1908. TS. Personal collection of the author.

—. Letter to Harvey M. Coverly, WPA Project Director. 3 Feb. 1943. TS. Archival
collection of National Archives. Newby Ely e-mailed papers to the author.
6 June 2012.

—. Letter to Selective Service Chairman. 1 Apr. 1942. TS. Personal collection of
the author.

—. *The Philippines.* N.d. TS. Personal collection of the author.

Rice, Marie. "Eulogy." 1964. TS. Personal collection of the author.

Rice, Robert. "Charles Freeman Rice." Collected papers. 1896-1957. MS.
Personal collection of Robert Rice, e-mailed to the author. 23 Apr. 2011.

—. Collected papers. 1888-2012. MS. Personal collection of Robert Rice,
e-mailed to the author. 16 Jan. 2012.

—. "Delight Rice." Collected papers. 1910-1923. MS. Personal collection of the
author. 13 Apr. 2011.

—. "Percy Eugene Rice." Collected papers. 1888-1959. MS. Personal collection
of Robert Rice, e-mailed to the author. 19 Jan. 2012.

Soriano, Rodolfo F. *History: SDB and PSD 1907-2007.* Collected papers.
1907-2007. MS. Personal collection of Rodolfo F. Soriano.
Ferdinand Deza e-mailed to the author. 11 Dec. 2007.

"Trio of Wisconsin's Helen Kellers." Illustration. 1904. TS. Archival collection of
Harvard University, Library of the Graduate School of Education.
Thomas Bull mailed to the author. 10 Jan. 2006.

"Unveiling of Marker During the PSD's Centennial Celebration." 2007. TS.
Archival collection of Philippine School for the Deaf Library.
Teacher Charo David e-mailed to the author. 14 Nov. 2011.

A Paper written by
Miss Delight Rice

On August 23, 1901, the U.S. Transport Thomas 'arrived in Manila,
P.I., with the men and women who took over from the Army, the work of
educating the Filipinos. These teachers were the material from which
the Bureau of Education was formed.

At the head of this bureau was a Director whose duty was to make
schools available for all children. In 1906, the Director was Dr.David
P. Barrows. Before going to the Philippines, Dr. Barrows had been a
professor at the University of California and had served on the Board
of Control of the State of California which had the California School
for the Deaf and Blind under its care.

With such experience for a background, it was natural that
Dr. Barrows should notice the exceptional children of the Philippines
as he travelled from island to island. The immediate cause for a special school was the blind son of a Filipino who was host to Dr.Barrows
on one of his inspection trips to the island of Panay. This boy sat
in a corner out of harm's way and nothing was done towards his school-
ing.A census was taken and it was reported that there were ninety-two
deaf and dumb persons in Manila and several thousand in the Provinces.
Upon the basis of this report, Dr. Barrows planned for the education
of both the deaf and blind.

Before selecting a teacher, there was the U. S. Civil Service
examination to be given. This was the regular test for all teachers
and only one question bothered me in geography; there was a long list
of places for location. Now no one denies that California and all its
possessions are among the best known in all the world, but I lived in
Ohio and Lake Tahoe meant nothing to me, so I put it in Africa. Great

Delight Rice's Typewritten Paper

May Delight Rice rest in peace.

HARRIET

CLARISSA C
HARRIS & PHEBE
HAWKINS

Index

**Rice Family Plot
at Five Corners Cemetery
in Milfordton Township,
Knox County, Ohio**

Index

Abat, Rafaelito (deaf Filipino researcher), 73
Advisory Commission on Special Education (George Attletweed as chairperson), 83
Alexander Graham Bell Association for the Deaf, 4
American Expeditionary Force Siberia (Delight as Red Cross nurse), 95, 129
American Sign Language (ASL), 73
Ansig, Datto (tribal headman for human sacrifice of deaf pupil), 45-47
Argila, Carl A. (SAID executive director), 72-73
Association of Parents, Teachers & Counselors (APTC), 85
Ateneo de Manila College (now University), 39, 80
Athletic meets, 59, 66
Attletweed, George (CSD and Gallaudet alumnus), 82-83, 130-131
Audiological testing, viii, 96-98, 101, 130

Barrows, David (Director of Philippine Bureau of Education), 28, 41
Barish, Joel (CSD legend), 78
Bay Area Asian Deaf Association (BAADA), 137
Bay Area Coalition of Deaf Senior Citizens (BACDSC), 85, 137
Bell, Alexander Graham, 94
Belting, Lucretia (last American SDB principal), 71, 141
Berkeley Public Schools, viii, 101-102, 130-131
Bernardo, Editha, 111
Blind classes, 56-57
Bohol Deaf Academy (BDA), 28
Boy Scouts of America (BSA)
  Troop 2, 58, 61, 67, 80
  Troop 11, 8, 84
Braille textbooks, 57
Brink, Gilbert (Assistant Director of Philippine Bureau of Education), 29

California Association of the Deaf (CAD), 83, 106-107
California Home for the Aged Deaf (CHAD), 107, 131
California News (CSD publication), 79-80, 103, 114
California School for the Deaf (CSD), viii-ix, xiii, xv, 8, 15, 74-85, 104-106, 121, 129-131, 137
California School for the Deaf Alumni Association (CSDAA), 83, 137
California School for the Deaf and Blind (CSDB), 8, 28-29, 78, 128
California School for the Deaf Historical Museum, vii, xv
Captioned Films, 113

Capulong, Yolanda (PSD principal), xii, 121-122, 133, 141
Central High School (CHS), 15, 127
College (now University) of the Pacific, ix, 107, 131
Colorado School for the Deaf, 85
Columbus Colony, 16
Columbus Normal School (CNS), 15, 127
Convention of American Instructors of the Deaf (CAID), 14, 20, 90-91, 127, 129
Crandall, H.B. (first deaf CSD teacher), 77
Cuengco, Bernardo (SDB and CSD alumnus), vii, xi, xv, 61, 80-81, 99-100, 114, 129-130
Cuengco, Rose Fong (Bernardo's wife), 81, 114

Davila, Robert (CSD legend), 77
Davis (now Daviton), Jeanette (CSD alumna), 84, 130-131
de Guzman, Maximiano (SDB alumnus), 112-113
Deaf Counseling, Advocacy & Referral Agency (DCARA), 83, 137
DEAF Media, 83, 137
Deaf Seniors of America (DSA), 136-137
d'Estrella, Theophilus (CSD legend), 77
Dial-A-News (DAN) (weekly news service), 83
Diki Diki, Paugliener (Moro dwarf), 86-87, 90
Drake, Dennis (IDEA founder), 28
Driggs, Mrs. Edwin (EBCD interpreter and advisor), 103-104
Dunick, Minnie (WSD deaf-blind student), 18-19

East Bay Club for the Deaf (EBCD), 81, 85, 103-104, 113, 131
East Bay Referral Agency for the Deaf, 83
Educational methods (Combined and oral methods), 50
Elstad, Leonard (Gallaudet College president), 85, 107-108

Fay, Edward Allen (Gallaudet College professor and vice-president), 4
Fay, Gilbert Otis (OSD superintendent), 4, 6, 127
Felizardo (later Gutierrez), Paula (Delight's first pupil), 31-32, 39, 79, 90, 129
Filipino Sign Language (FSL), 73
Final farewell, 61
Fisher, John (IDEA founder), 28
Five Corners Cemetery, 8, 114, 160-162
Fletcher, Harvey (Audiometer and hearing aid inventor), 101
Forbes, W. Cameron (Philippine governor-general), 58
Francisco, Maria (First native PSD principal), 72, 141

Gaertner, George W. (Reverend), 103
Galang, Emmanuel and Maricris (PSD alumni), 121-122
Gallaudet, Edward Miner (Gallaudet College president), 14, 22
Gallaudet, Thomas Hopkins, 94
Gallaudet College (now University), viii-x, xiii, 4-5, 8, 22, 27, 79-82, 84-85, 107-108, 127, 131, 134-135, 137
Gallaudet University Library and Archives, vii, xv
Gore, W.E. (Host for Alice Rice), 92
Gough School for the Oral Deaf, 100, 130

Halliday, Eva (WSD deaf-blind student), 17-19, 23
Hall, Percival (Gallaudet College president), 90-91
Hanson, Agatha Tiegel, 107-108
Harrison, Francis B. (Philippine governor-general), 92
Hayes, Julia (2nd American SDB principal), 71-72, 141
Hearing Center of Metropolitan Los Angeles (HCMLA), 106-107, 131-132
Helen Keller School, 104-105
Hirano Family
Hirano, Ronald (CSD and Gallaudet alumnus, vii-xiii, xv, 83-85, 104-108, 113-114, 121-122, 130-131, 134-137
Father: Hirano, James Shigeo, 83, 105-106, 137
Mother: Hirano, Mary Shizue, 83, 105, 137
Brother: Hirano, Robert, xv, 105, 137
Sister: Hirano (now Matsuoka), Janet Inako, 105
Brother: Hirano, Daniel, 105
Sister: Hirano, Carol Aiko, xv, 105
Brother: Hirano, Gordon Rice, 137
Hom, Chuck (CSD and Gallaudet alumnus), 121
Horticulture, 65

International Deaf Education Association (IDEA), 28

Jaime, Infante (Duke of Segovia), 90, 129
Japanese occupation, vii, 72
Johnson, Anna (WSD deaf-blind student), 18-19, 93

Kendall School, 79
Klopping, Henry (CSD superintendent), xiii, 121-122, 133

Lagman, Francisca (SDB teacher), 39-40, 43-44, 51, 78-79, 128
Lagman, Rogerio (First blind teacher at SDB), 39-40, 44, 56-57, 78, 128
Lankenau, Robert (NAD president), 79
Lipreading, 85, 100, 102, 130
Lopez, Vincente, 111
Luzon Association of the Deaf, 112
Lynch, Daniel (CSD and Gallaudet alumnus), 84, 130-131

Manila Institute for the Deaf and Dumb (later SDB), 39
Manila Bullentin, 150
Manila Times, 108
Manzanar Internment Camp, 105
Maps
California, 144
Central Ohio, 145
Metro Manila, 147
Ohio, 145
Philippine Islands, 146
San Francisco Bay Area, 144
United States of America, 144
World, 142-143
Martinez, Liza (Philippine Deaf Resource Center director), 73
Meyers, Wildey (California News writer), 103
Miriam College, 27
Momii, Kazuko "Kay" (CSD and Utah School for the Deaf alumna), 106

Naftaly, Lester (SDB, CSD and Gallaudet alumnus), 61, 80-82, 99-100, 129-130
Naftaly, Jennie Ghera (Lester's first wife), 82
Naftaly, Norma Lose Hensley (Lester's second wife), 82
National Association of the Deaf (NAD), 79, 93
National Fraternal Society of the Deaf (NFSD), 89
Ner, Anita Ortiz (PSD and SAID alumna), xv, 121
New York School for the Deaf (Fanwood), 77
North Carolina School for the Deaf, 14, 20, 127

Ohio Chronicle (OSD publication), 50, 148
Ohio Home for the Aged and Infirm Deaf (now Columbus Colony), 16
Ohio School for the Deaf (OSD), vii-viii, 5-7, 15-17, 21-22, 50, 127
Ohlone College, 83-84
OSD Alumni Association (OSDAA), 16, 127

Pacheco, Florentino, 111
Papa, Sergio (Delight's first successful student), 31
Parsons, Frances (Gallaudet University professor), 27, 79
Peace Corps, 27-28
Pecson, Paula (SDB industrial teacher), 49
Philippine Association of the Deaf (PAD), vii, 79-81, 90, 110, 113, 132
Philippine Citizen (Pedro Santos' California News articles), 79
Philippine Deaf Resource Center, 73
Philippine National School for the Blind, 73, 119
Philippine Normal School (now University), 29, 33, 39-40, 46, 128
Philippine School for the Deaf (PSD), vi-vii, xii-xiii, 73, 116-121, 123, 123-134, 137, 141
Pure oral method, 72-73

Reception for government officials, 58
Redmond, Granville (CSD legend), 77
Rice family
 Rice, Delight, vi-xiii, xv, xvii (1), 4, 6-7, 11,
   13-23, 25, 29-33, 38-47, 49-51, 56-61, 67,
   71, 73, 78-85, 89-91, 93-117, 121-133, 135,
   137, 141
 Father: Rice, Charles Merrick, x, 4-7, 56, 65,
   68-70, 72, 88-90, 92, 94-95, 100, 102-103,
   127, 129-130
 Mother: Rice, Alice Isadora Gregg, 4, 6, 65,
   86-90, 92-93, 95, 127, 129
 Brother: Rice, George Merrick, 4, 6
 Brother: Rice, Percy Eugene, vii, x, xv, 4, 6-8, 89,
   92
 Percy's first wife: Rice, Ester Louella Sutten, 7
 Nephew: Rice, Charles "Buddy" Sutton, x, 7, 9,
   11, 114
 Percy's second wife: Rice, Leda Rosemond Fife, 7
 Nephew: Rice, Robert Eugene, vii, x-xi, 7, 10-11,
   114
 Brother: Rice, Charles Freeman, x, 6-8, 80,
   88-89, 92-93
Rice-Gregg grandparents
 Grandfather: Rice, James Chandler, 5
 Grandmother: Rice, Martha Ann Hawkins, 5, 7
 Grandfather: Gregg, John, 6
 Grandmother: Gregg, Cecelia Delight
   Alexander, 6-7
Ripley, John Porter (OSD deaf-blind student), 21
Roger, Edward (SDB alumnus), vii

Saami, Roy (Blake Street resident), xi
San Francisco Club for the Deaf (SFCD), 113
San Francisco State University (SFSU), 83, 85, 137
Santos, Pedro (SDB, CSD and Kendall School
   alumnus), 32, 79-80, 129
School for the Deaf and the Blind or SDB (now
   Philippine School for the Deaf)
 Ermita School, 35-47, 128
 Intramuros School, 34, 48-51, 128
 Port District School, 34, 49, 52-67, 128
 Pasay School, 68-73, 110, 113, 130, 132-133
School for the Deaf Alumni Association, 110,
   112-113, 132
School for the Deaf at Tokyo, 94
School groups, 62-63

Senior Quest (BACDSC publication), 85
Separation of the school (SDB and PSD-PNSB),
   73
Silent Perspectives (Emmy Award-winning weekly
   television program), 83
Silent Worker (Deaf national publication), 60, 94,
   108, 149
Smith, Stanley (CSD/Gallaudet alumnus and
   teacher), 121-122, 133
Soriano, Isauro (SDB alumnus), 113
Southeast Asia Institute for the Deaf (SAID), 27,
   72, 121
SouthWest Collegiate Institute for the Deaf
   (SWCID), 84
Sports, 66
Stanford University, 100

Takagi, Ruth (CSD alumna), 105
Tanforan Assembly Center, 104, 131
Teaching methods (Deaf-blind), 19
Thomasites, 27
Tilden, Douglas (CSD legend), 76-77
Topaz Internment Camp, 105-106, 131
Tule Lake Internment Camp, 104-105

U.S. Special Census on Deaf Family, Marriage
   and Hearing Relatives, 1888-1895, 4
University of California (UC), 9-10, 28, 83
Utah School for the Deaf, 106

Virginia School for the Deaf, 90-91, 129
Virnig, Sean (CSD legend), 78
Vocational training, 57-58, 64
Volta Bureau, 4
Vukotić, Dragoljub "Drago" (WFD president), 113

Walker, E.W. (WSD superintendent), 20
Webber, Ralph (Delight's former husband), 89, 129
West, Richard (SDB alumnus), vii, 90, 110, 112-
   113, 131
Wisconsin School for the Deaf (WSD), vii-viii,
   12-13, 16-21, 23, 89, 127
Wood, Leonard (Philippine governor-general), 61,
   80
World Federation of the Deaf (WFD), 113

Yamamoto, Tadashi "Tad" (CSD alumnus), 104

North Tower of
Golden Gate Bridge
San Francisco, California

Catherine "Kay" and Ronald Hirano

Sayonara